THE
SECRET
POWER
WITHIN

Also by Chuck Norris
The Secret of Inner Strength: My Story

THE SECRET POWER WITHIN

Zen solutions to real problems

by

CHUCK NORRIS

BROADWAY BOOKS
New York

It is better to light a candle than curse
the gathering darkness

--Zen saying

BROADWAY

This book was originally published in 1996 by Little, Brown & Company.
It is here reprinted by arrangement with Little, Brown & Company.

THE SECRET POWER WITHIN. Copyright © 1996 by Top Kick Productions.
All rights reserved. Printed in the United States of America. No part of this book
may be reproduced or transmitted in any form or by any means, electronic or
mechanical, including photocopying, recording, or by any information storage and
retrieval system, without written permission from the publisher. For information
address Broadway Books, a division of Bantam Doubleday Dell
Publishing Group, Inc., 1540 Broadway, New York, NY 10036.

Broadway Books titles may be purchased for
business or promotional use or for special sales.
For information, please write to: Special Markets Department, Bantam
Doubleday Dell Publishing Group, Inc., 1540 Broadway, New York, NY 10036.

BROADWAY BOOKS and its logo, a letter B bisected
on the diagonal, are trademarks of Broadway Books,
a division of Bantam Doubleday Dell
Publishing Group, Inc.

Library of Congress Cataloging-in-Publication Data
Norris, Chuck, 1940-
The secret power within : Zen solutions to real problems / by Chuck Norris. —
1st Broadway Books ed.
p. cm.
Originally published: 1st ed. Boston : Little, Brown & Co., c1996.
ISBN 0-553-06908-X (pbk.)
1. Martial arts. 2. Zen Buddhism and martial arts. 3. Norris, Chuck, 1940-
I. Title.
[GV1102.N67 1997]
769.8—dc20   96-31801
CIP

FIRST BROADWAY BOOKS EDITION PUBLISHED 1997

97 98 99 00 01 10 9 8 7 6 5 4 3 2 1

CONTENTS

THE
SECRET
POWER
WITHIN

PREFACE

My first experience with Zen was in 1962 in Torrance, California. I was a young black belt and I had just started a martial arts school, which was one of the first in the Los Angeles area. The school, located in what had been a store, was right on the corner of two main streets. Cars passing by would slow down to look through the big windows, and people would often just walk in off the street to watch the classes for a while — a karate class was something unusual back then. From time to time a monk wearing the saffron robes of a Buddhist would drop by. I'd see him come in, be aware of him sitting there quietly watching me teach my students, and then I'd look up to find that he was gone.

One day, at the end of a session, I went over to talk with him before he could leave. I learned he was from the Yogananda temple in downtown Los Angeles and that he, too, was a martial artist. The fact that we were both martial artists made him feel a certain kinship with me, and he had a lot he wanted to share. As we chatted, he mentioned the word *ki* several times, which he described as an internal force and said was related to Zen.

Zen: Today that little word has been reduced to a kind of catchphrase that can be attached to everything from learning to use the Internet to getting ahead in the business world. It has been detached from its original source so thoroughly that its meaning, at least for a great many people, has become a matter of personal conjecture. I doubt it would be used quite so often if people had to use its full name, Zen Buddhism, which is what the monk was talking about.

Although I had earned my black belt while I was in the air force in Korea I knew nothing about Zen. My Korean instructor had rarely mentioned it, at least not that I was aware of, for he spoke very little English, and although he could make himself understood when need be, he was most comfortable with a series of shouted commands. I'd heard of ki, however, but it seemed vaguely mysterious, almost magical. And here was this monk talking about it as though it were something nearby.

Curious to learn more about both Zen and ki, I asked the monk more questions. He said, "Let's step on the mat [training area]."

My students for the day were gone, so I locked the front door and faced him on the mat.

"Kneel down and close your eyes," he said, "and concentrate on the third eye, which is between and slightly above your eyes. Focus on that third eye and concentrate."

I knelt on the floor, closed my eyes, and staring into that blackness I soon saw a dark spot about the size of a dime that was starting to get brighter.

As I was kneeling there, the monk told me more about ki.

From what he said I understood only that ki was some kind of universal force, everywhere around us, and that certain people were able to make use of it. He told me stories about the exploits of various monks and warriors in the fourteenth and fifteenth centuries, stories that involved using the power of ki. One of the stories was about a samurai who was set upon in the woods by a pack of wolves, but he just kept walking straight ahead, his countenance so stable, so self-aware yet potentially explosive that the animals were frozen in their tracks, and he passed safely through their midst. Another was about men lying in ambush to confront a victim who simply by gazing at them terrorized them so effectively that they were immobilized. While he was telling me these stories, the dark spot became as bright as the sun.

The monk finally told me to open my eyes, and when I did so, it was like waking up: I discovered I'd been kneeling on the mat for four hours. When I tried to get up I felt excruciating pain — the circulation in my legs had been cut off. The monk massaged my legs until the blood was flowing again. Then he said good-bye. After that experience, I went to the Yogananda temple in Los Angeles several times. The monk tried to convince me to convert, but my Christian faith was too strong.

But that was when I first became aware that there was more to the martial arts than just the physical, and it was a turning point in my life. I've spoken to various people about that monk and the "third eye," and I can't say I've ever had a satisfactory explanation. But it was my first experience with Zen, and weird as it was, it piqued my curiosity.

That was more than thirty years ago, and over the years my understanding of that other side of the martial arts has grown considerably. In the end, the idea of a third eye helps in an understanding of Zen, since Zen is another way of seeing — you could even say a way of seeing with both your eyes closed.

This book is about what I've seen and understood by looking through Zen. It's about my life and the lives of people I've known, about real-life experiences that are in some way related to Zen or that make a special kind of sense when looked at in Zen terms. A lot of the stories here are from my background as a martial artist, because the arts and Zen are closely related. I entered Zen through the martial arts, beginning with the monk in his saffron robes, but studying martial arts is certainly not the only way to come to an understanding of Zen.

Some people come to Zen suddenly; after all, in its purest form, Zen is usually understood not just as "enlightenment," but as "sudden enlightenment," something like waking up from a deep sleep or from a deep "distraction," meaning, waking up from the superficial confusions of this world. The stories of Zen adepts (experts) who have achieved such sudden awakenings are exciting to read and say a lot not just about Zen but about what Zen can mean today, how it can fit into our world. And it really does fit. People have reached enlightenment riding to work in a van crowded with carpoolers; some have reached enlightenment while shaving or leaning over to pick up a newspaper.

Enlightenment is real and is within our grasp all the time; at any moment we may awaken from our current perception of the world around us to another view altogether. With such enlightenment, nothing changes except our point of view, and that changes everything forever.

I don't know what total enlightenment would be like, but

I've had glimpses, and such glimpses are what I offer here. These are views into what is really happening in life, suggestions for finally agreeing on the meaning of success and happiness and for recognizing them when they come. After reading this book, you should come away with an increased understanding of Zen and how its thinking can improve your life and enable you to take and fully experience those first steps toward increased awareness. With all of its age-old power and wisdom, all of its experience and deep compassion, Zen wants you to find yourself. Zen actively wants you to achieve happiness and be content with your life. Enlightenment is the goal, it is the future; but just deciding to take the right steps, just facing in the right direction, can have a powerful impact on today, on how you live your life every moment from now on. There can be no doubt that Zen can be applied to any life — Zen can be entered by anyone, anywhere — and I'm convinced that the application will always be beneficial, since Zen begins and ends at the most human level, with how people think of themselves and others. The first decision is simply to let Zen help you, let it do what it is designed to do. And that isn't hard. The only requirement is you yourself: You are all that you will ever need in order to begin.

Looking at Zen with a completely open mind is essential; and with traditional Zen irony, I could add that one possible purpose of Zen is to open your mind. Zen is like that: The ideas roll and turn in on themselves. To give a sense of that aspect of Zen, I've included some of my favorite Zen stories and aphorisms in this book, most of them ancient, some of them modern reworkings of older tales. Although many of these bits of Zen wisdom have something to say about life, their purpose is not to teach lessons, at least not in our usual Western sense. In fact, it's important to realize that there are no right or wrong answers to Zen questions. The object of all these stories and aphorisms is to make you move your mind, use your mind, in the same way as a physical exercise makes you move and use your body. If you keep at Zen long enough, trying to work out questions that have no "correct" answer, you'll find yourself able to move your mind in new ways and you'll gradually find yourself in possession of new strengths with which you can expand your mental horizons.

An important aspect of Zen that I've come to value is that it teaches us that we're not alone. At heart, we all want the same thing, whether we call it "enlightenment," "happiness," or "love." Too many people spend their lives waiting for that something to arrive — and that's not the Zen way. Zen is always on the side of action, always on the side of doing whatever is necessary and right, so that people can live rewarding lives. Within Zen, we all share a certain kinship.

In writing this book I've had to look back over my life. I've come to realize that although the many steps I took to arrive at the present now seem inevitable, even obvious, the truth is, at the time, each step could have gone another way. Sometimes it was like a compass needle spinning, and I had to somehow locate my own personal north. In this book I try to show the way I came into Zen and how I applied it as I moved through life, but I don't necessarily mean for you to follow me, to take the same route I took, or even to look at Zen in the same way. Rather, I suggest you move ahead with Zen following your own route, beginning now.

I am a contemporary man, not a Zen master, but I put this book forward with the belief that it will help others apply Zen, or at least the wisdom behind Zen, to real-life situations. Any such application will be subtle and only a matter of interpretation, of course. Books about Zen are widely regarded as useless; according to that line of reasoning, Zen cannot be understood from the outside, from the point of view of an observer, regardless of how eager to learn that observer might be.

I would probably agree with that in principle. When Westerners encounter actual examples of Zen, they often come away confused, if not disappointed. A tea ceremony can be an act of Zen, as can flower arranging, calligraphy, or archery. And what happens? The tea master never seems to get around to actually pouring the tea; the flower arranger puts more effort into untying the bunches of flowers than into arranging them; the calligrapher dedicates most of his energy to preparing his various brushes; and although the archer makes convincing movements with his bow, he seems completely oblivious to such matters as aiming at his target — he doesn't seem to care whether or not he even hits it.

But he hits it, just as the calligrapher ultimately creates a beautiful and harmonious page. Learning to see each of those arts, like the martial arts, as a ceremony is to begin to understand. Coming to see beyond the ceremony to the practice and dedication, the respect and discipline, that makes an art possible is to reach an even deeper understanding.

The sure aim of the archer and the quick touch of the calligrapher may seem unrelated to our day-to-day lives; but the Zen that inwardly powers those movements, that makes them possible in the first place, can be applied everywhere by everyone who wishes to develop the secret power within, a power we all have.

YOU CAN GET THERE
FROM HERE

If we don't change the direction we are going, we
are likely to end up where we are heading.

— *Chinese saying*

I've never been psychoanalyzed, but I imagine that if I were,
the analyst would probably begin with my early childhood
memories and be as puzzled as I am about the course of my
life. I was raised in a small clapboard house on the outskirts
of Wilson, Oklahoma, a small prairie town, flat, dusty, and
arid, with a population of about one thousand souls. Wilson
is just a few miles east of the Texas border, bound by poverty
and desolation on all sides. When locals talked about leaving Wilson for greener pastures, the usual response was "You
can't get there from here." Be that as it may, I am proof that
you *can* get there from here.

As a toddler I shared a pallet on the floor with my younger
brother Wieland, and Mom bathed us together in a big gal-
vanized tin washtub. Our toilet was an outhouse. I hated that

outhouse so much that I used to walk two miles to my aunt's house to use her facilities.

I can remember riding high up on my father's shoulders and looking out over the Red River toward the Texas side. He was busy stringing fishing lines, and I must have been happy at that moment because it's one of the few vivid and good memories I have of time spent with him.

When I flash back on that scene now, it seems like an image I saw in some movie: father and son on a riverbank with fishing lines stabbed out over shining water — a perfect image of family togetherness. I have my own sons now, and I know what it's like to be the father. I can remember picking them up and putting them on my shoulders, when they were little. And while they were up on my shoulders they probably thought to themselves how great that was. I suspect that, like me as a child, they probably thought that someday they'd be that tall, even taller than their father. Riding on your father's shoulders is a way of measuring your future, getting an idea of how big a man you'll be.

The sad truth is that my father was not a good measure of a man, and my few good memories of him are overwhelmed and nearly blotted out by other memories of him coming home drunk or simply not being around when he was needed.

When my dad came back from World War II he had a bad leg and a drinking problem that would eventually cause his death some years later. My father didn't offer me any kind of role model to follow, but my mother more than made up for that. Her inner strength and simple wisdom — her belief system — shaped my character. She believed in determination and patience: the determination to succeed in whatever you choose to do in your life, and the patience to stick with it until the goal is reached. She had no awareness of Zen, had probably never heard the word, but her philosophy was practical, which is what Zen is.

Apart from my mother, my only role models were the cowboy heroes I saw on the screen in the movie theater in Wilson. I spent most of my Saturday afternoons there when my mother could afford the admission price. The Westerns I saw starring men like Gary Cooper, John Wayne, Randolph Scott, and Joel McCrea provided me with plenty of positive examples for proper and moral behavior. Each time I walked out of a theater after a Saturday matinee, I felt empowered with the belief that there were such men and the dream that I might grow up one day to be like them. Some people today find fault with those old-time heroes and consider them corny, but the truth is they had a lot to offer a young boy eager for lessons in life. Their behavior in each film was governed by the "Code of the West": loyalty, friendship, and integrity. They taught me about not being selfish, about doing what is right even when the risk is great. Years later I would remember those Western heroes when I was trying to work out the kind of character I wanted to play as an actor, but in those days I was only a spectator involved in vicarious adventure.

In school I was shy and inhibited: When I knew it was going to be my turn to recite something aloud in front of the class, I usually found an excuse to be absent. Although I was an average student and a fair athlete, I was content to fade into the background, although all the time I had a dream, to be like one of those heroes on the silver screen.

We were dirt poor, and Dad changed jobs so often that we had moved thirteen times by the time I was fifteen years old. He drove a Greyhound bus for a while, worked as a truck driver, and finally landed a menial job with Bethlehem Steel in

Hawthorne, California, where the four of us lived in a twenty-foot-long house trailer parked on my aunt's empty back lot. It stood out like a sore thumb in the middle of the field. We were so poor that one time when I was in the fifth grade and the teacher wanted to measure our height, I was ashamed to take my boots off because I had such big holes in my socks. Later, in high school, I met a girl I liked, but when she asked to meet my mother, I broke up with her rather than have her see where and how we lived.

At that period of my life I had no aspirations to a good or even a better life than what I saw around me, despite my mother's insistence that my two brothers and I could do anything we wanted with our lives if we were patient and worked hard. I still had dreams about being like one of my cowboy heroes when I was older: I tried to pattern my behavior after them, but back then I never realized I could be one of them someday.

My parents divorced in 1956, when I was sixteen, and a little more than a year later my mother married George Knight, a foreman at Northrop Aircraft, where she worked. Although George had three kids of his own, he treated us all as though we were one family. I finally had a father who was a good role model, and I began to come out of my shell, to realize that maybe I had a chance to change the direction of my life.

After school and on Saturdays I worked as a box boy for Boy's market, but my self-image then was still based on those movies I had seen as a kid in Oklahoma: I wanted to be a policeman. With that in mind, I enlisted in the air force after graduating from high school so I could get into the military police and gain some experience in police work. The air force sent me to

Korea, and at the age of eighteen, I left behind a wife and an uncertain future.

Looking back, I realize that was *the* turning point in my life, because it was while I was in Osan, Korea, that I started to study martial arts. For the first time I began to see at least part of my childhood dream as a possible reality, and I had a consuming passion to learn something, although I had no idea then where it would lead. But, as the Zen masters say, the longest journey begins with the first step, and, unknowingly, I had taken the first step leading to my future.

At the start I was interested only in learning something that would help me as a military policeman. By the time I left Korea, I had a black belt in *tae kwon do,* a Korean martial art, and for the first time in my life I had confidence in my ability to pursue something to the end: I had finally succeeded on my own in a truly difficult undertaking, and I had thereby gained some self-esteem.

After being discharged from the air force, I had to face the practical reality of earning a living for my family — our son Mike was born in October 1962 — so I took the only job I could get, working as a file clerk in records management at Northrop for a salary of $240 a month. But I still had the dream of changing the direction of my life.

To supplement my income, I began to teach karate in my parents' backyard to my brothers and friends. Soon, the word spread in the neighborhood that my karate classes were fun and the self-defense lessons learned might be useful in daily life. To earn a reputation for myself, and perhaps get more students, I started to compete successfully in karate tournaments around the state, and later around the country. As I had hoped, once I began to earn a reputation as a karate fighter, my school began to prosper. Soon I had students enough to encourage me to open up more schools.

As I became more successful in karate tournaments, I realized that in order to be a champion — which would help me get even more students — I would have to learn more, so I began to study and share ideas with the masters active in the West Coast area and those I met on the tournament circuit. That, too, was an important step, for kicks and punches — details of technique — were only a small part of what I learned. My horizons were gradually expanding; I was becoming aware of my possibilities — not just possibilities for a better personal life but possibilities for taking a more active part in the larger world around me. Zen was an important aspect of this, for through those years of study, I came to understand that behind every martial art is a philosophy, usually Zen or a system similar to Zen. The philosophy is an integral part of the learning process.

The learning experience is subtle and gradual, because to truly learn a martial art requires as much use of the brain as the body. The real lessons of martial arts aren't kicks and punches but rather the calm self-assurance that comes from feeling good about yourself, certain of who you are and what you hope to accomplish, and the way to reach your goal.

I can't present an overview of the important steps and events of my life without talking about the death of my brother Wieland, who was killed in action in Vietnam in June 1970. Wieland was my best friend, and we shared our dreams for the future, a future he would never have. More than any other event, his death made me aware of my real responsibilities to not just my own personal goals but to the hopes and feelings of the people around me, the members of my family and, in truth, the other people in this country. Wieland's death locked me into an awareness of contemporary realities, of the country in which we live and of this time in history.

Wieland died fighting for his country. He died in accordance with the values and ideals he and I were brought up with, ideas we talked about and thought about together as boys. Those values and ideals have a solid meaning, a real application in this world. I knew that all along, of course, but Wieland's death forced me to overcome my natural shyness so that I could speak out loud. By the time I found myself acting in movies, I had determined what kind of hero I wanted to present, based on the cowboy heroes of my childhood. I knew the character I wanted to adopt in order to pass those values and ideals on to others.

The martial arts are only one aspect of that character; they're a vehicle for exciting action, for moving the story along. But the martial artist as a hero has something else to offer, a philosophy of life that includes a code of behavior and moral obligations to others. John Wayne and other Western heroes had a philosophy of right and wrong and the means to implement it, namely, their courage and their skill with weapons. Today's heroes need the same qualities, but with certain differences. In the final fight scene of a contemporary martial arts film, all the weapons — guns, swords, whatever — are knocked aside, out of reach, leaving the opponents with only their empty hands. It's a symbolism I like, because in the end that's how we all have to face the problems that beset us: When our hands are empty, what will decide the fight is what's inside our minds.

ZEN IS WHERE YOU
FIND IT

A young man came to a Zen master and asked, "I have come here seeking the Truth. Where can I start to get into Zen?"

The master asked, "Can you hear the murmuring of the mountain stream?"

"Yes, I can hear it," said the young man.

"Enter Zen from there!"

— Zen tale

I began entering Zen from Oklahoma, which is to say, I was born nowhere near a Zen monastery. The people I grew up around had far more in common with a tale by Mark Twain than with the sayings of Confucius. I had never heard of Zen until I was serving in Korea in the air force. At first it was just a word, and later, when I came to understand something of its meaning, it never occurred to me to go sit outside a monastery waiting to be admitted. I never considered that, because by the time I learned the meaning of Zen, I knew I was already entering it.

The truth is that getting into Zen can be hard, if not absolutely impossible, if you go at it the wrong way. If you presented yourself at the door of a Zen monastery in Japan and requested instruction in Zen, you'd be turned away — perhaps politely, perhaps not. You'd be told that the school was already crowded and that there was no room for you. Or you'd be told that the school was poor and couldn't afford another student. Or you'd be told some other story. The only certainty is that you wouldn't be allowed to pass through the door.

At least not immediately, and probably not the first day. This refusal at the door is part of the tradition. In fact, it's the first lesson of Zen and is designed to turn away all but the truly dedicated. And the aspiring student must endure more than waiting outside the door: In most cases he or she must also undergo verbal abuse from the monks — "What, are you still here? Didn't we tell you to go away? Go!" — and the lack of food and water. But if you waited outside the door long enough, enduring the long hours, the taunts, and the hunger, you would probably be asked to come inside. Eventually.

And once you got past the door? You might be instructed to sit in a corner, in which case you'd find yourself abandoned and ignored. Or you might be immediately given a chore to do, something you'd never done before in your life — cut kindling, start the fire under the bath, fix the roof tiles — with no information offered on how to go about the chore, not even a hint as to where the proper tools might be. Most likely, you'd be given three or four things to do at once, with nothing about tools, nothing about the order in which the chores should be performed. No guidance or help whatsoever.

That's how your Zen training might begin. That certainly is how it began for students in the past, many of whom later wrote about the experience. I remember the story of one man — who later became a famous Zen master — who was made to wait three days in cold rain. And when he looked back on that experience later in life he saw not cruelty, but compassion.

Had the monks at the monastery door shaken his hand gladly, patted him on the back, taken him inside, and offered him a cup of tea, would they have been preparing him for life? Would they have been helping him achieve enlightenment? To outsiders Zen sometimes seems cold and completely unsentimental. To those who have come inside, whether through the front door, a mountain stream, or karate, it seems honest and human — and both of those things overwhelmingly.

I've always been struck by the strong resemblance between those first steps of Zen and life itself. If you really want something, you must go after it yourself, and with all your dedication: No one is going to give it to you, and if you waver or doubt, you're sure to fail. And what could be a better imitation of life than finding yourself faced with the responsibility for performing a series of chores, things you've never done before, without advance warning, without prior instruction, and without guidance or help? And sometimes in life you find yourself alone and ignored in the rain.

THE TASTE OF ZEN

We are what we think:

All that we are arises

With our thoughts.

With our thoughts

We make the world.

— Buddha

Zen is everywhere in the Orient, especially in China and Japan. The poetry, calligraphy, and painting of those countries are said to reflect Zen, and in the same way Zen is the creative discipline behind flower arranging, garden landscaping — those famous rock gardens — archery, and most aspects of daily life, including the tea ceremony. And, of course, Zen is integral to the Oriental martial arts, because it is not only a philosophy but it suggests a right way of conducting one's life.

Knowing where Zen is supposed to be doesn't help you find it or understand it, because as soon as you start looking for

Zen, it disappears or seems to become something so vague that no one can talk about it. But writing poetry and painting a picture, creating a work of calligraphy, arranging a garden, even performing the rituals of the tea ceremony do have something in common in that they're based on discipline.

But Zen is obviously more than that. One of my favorite sayings about Zen is that the taste of Zen is the same as the taste of tea. It's a typical Zen saying, deceptively simple but capable of suggesting various interpretations. Zen tastes like tea because it stimulates the body the way tea does: It clarifies the mind and wakes you up. It wakes you up to yourself and to your surroundings. So the taste of Zen is a heightened sense of awareness, so that you can see the beauty and simplicity of even the most ordinary things.

Zen stories and aphorisms, most of them very old and handed down over the generations, offer some insight into the true meaning of Zen because they illuminate in roundabout ways. One of my favorites — probably because I'm a martial artist — involves a young man who wanted to learn the art of sword fighting. He hiked up into the mountains to a famous old sword master who had retired to live out his last years in a hut. The master agreed to take on the student, and the student went to live with him there on the mountain. From the very beginning, the master found plenty of things for the student to do: gather kindling, split wood, make fires, cook rice, draw water from the spring, sweep out the rooms, clean up the garden, and so on. Days and weeks went by, and still the master said nothing about either swords or swordsmanship; instead, every morning the student found himself facing his daily series of chores. Finally, the student got tired of being the old man's servant and of not learning anything about the art of the sword. So he approached the master and asked him about the teaching he had come for. The master agreed, and the student went back to his chores.

But the lessons had begun. Just as the student began to cook rice early the next morning, the master suddenly appeared behind him, whacked him with a wooden sword, and disappeared without saying a word. The student then began sweeping out the rooms. And at a certain moment, when he least expected it, the master was there right beside him again, hit him again with the sword, and disappeared. This went on all day, every day. No matter what the student was doing, he could never be at rest, knowing that at any moment the master would again appear and hit him with the wooden sword.

A few years went by this way — at least according to the version of the story I like, by D. T. Suzuki — and eventually the student learned to successfully dodge the master's blow no matter which angle it came from. The student felt he had accomplished something, but the master was not satisfied with him yet.

Then one morning, the student spotted the master busy cooking some vegetables over an open fire. The student decided to turn the tables, picked up a big stick, and crept up on the master. When the master stooped over the cooking pot, the student raised the stick and swung it down on the master — who in an instant grabbed the cover off the cooking pot, spun around, and used it to catch the tip of the stick.

In that moment the student had the kind of sudden insight Zen is famous for: He saw into one of the secrets of the art of sword fighting, that sensory awareness has to be developed to the point that one can anticipate movement as well as thought. He also learned that one must always have an open mind ready to learn at all times. And, for the first time, the young student understood and deeply appreciated the kindness of his master.

Learning any martial art involves the step-by-step memorization and perfection of movements and techniques, but all the technical skills in the world can't create a great martial artist and, in fact, will mean nothing if they aren't applied to a mind receptive to their use. The sword master could have taught the student lessons in how to hold the sword, various techniques of footwork, parries, and thrusts, but those lessons would have been empty and meaningless.

Instead, he taught him the frame of mind necessary to a great swordsman, the frame of mind in which the swordsman is completely attuned to his surroundings, ready at any moment to respond. The other lessons could come later, for the student had learned something of what can be called the Zen of swordsmanship.

WINNING BY
YIELDING

I first saw jujitsu, although I didn't know it at the time, in a movie entitled *Think Fast, Mr. Moto,* starring Peter Lorre as an importer and private detective involved in cracking a smuggling case. In one scene the diminutive Mr. Moto (Lorre) flipped a large man over his shoulder with remarkable, almost magical, ease. From that day on, I made it a point to see each of the seven subsequent films about Mr. Moto's adventures, waiting impatiently for the obligatory scene when Mr. Moto effortlessly tossed a big man around. I was never disappointed, and always astounded.

Years later when I took basic infantry training, I discovered that Mr. Moto had been doing something called *jujitsu,* an ancient Japanese martial art that gives a small man a decided advantage over a larger opponent. The essence of traditional jujitsu is that you should use the energy and strength of your opponent and turn it against him. The jujitsu expert is as elusive as the truth of Zen: He must make himself into a *koan,* a puzzle that slips away the more one tries to solve it. In short, he should be like water that falls through the fingers of those who try to clutch it, for the moment the fingers begin to close it moves away, not by its own strength, but by using the pressure applied to it.

According to legend, jujitsu was first discovered through watching the snow fall on the branches of trees. On the branches of tough and rigid trees the snow piles up until they crack beneath its weight, while thin and springy branches simply yield and drop the snow on the ground without being broken or bent.

Until recently jujitsu, arguably the first of the martial arts (it dates back to the Edo period in Japan), had fallen into the cracks between the proliferating other more popular Asian fighting arts.

Now, however, it is in the forefront of the martial arts, thanks to the expertise of various members of the Gracies and Machados, a family of Brazilians who have developed a formidable style of jujitsu. It gained prominence through their appearances on *The Ultimate Challenge,* a television show in which martial artists from all over the world — each with his unique style — compete in a round-robin in which the winner faces a member of the Gracie family. To date, the Gracies have never lost a match — not here, and never in their homeland.

Gracie jujitsu was developed and refined by Carlos Gracie Sr., who trained under a Japanese nobleman in Brazil and went on to found his own system and dynasty, which includes brothers and cousins, all of whom are experts.

I first heard of the Gracies in 1987 when I was scuba diving off an island in Brazil with Bob Wall, who co-starred with Bruce Lee and me in *Enter the Dragon.* After our vacation, Bob and I went to Rio de Janeiro to check out the martial arts schools. We worked out at several tae kwon do and capoiera schools. *Capoiera* is a devastating self-defense system with emphasis on leg and head-butting techniques that was founded more than three hundred years ago by African slaves and banned by the government for most of its history.

The instructors at the schools told us about the Gracie jujitsu system and how everyone feared their practitioners. Bob and I arranged to meet with Helio Gracie, the younger brother of Carlos Gracie Sr., and Helio's sons Rickson, the world champion, and Royce. They invited us to work out with them.

I felt some confidence in my ability to handle myself on the ground because I had studied grappling techniques for many years with Gene LeBell, a former judo and wrestling champion who, in my opinion, is one of the finest martial artists in the world. I had started studying with Gene because most real fights end up on the ground.

The moment Rickson and I began grappling, my years of experience went out the window. Rickson countered every move I made with a choke hold that caused me to submit instantly. I had never experienced that before other than when grappling with Gene.

Bob and I trained with the Gracies for several days until it was time to return home. Three years later, my good friend Richard Norton, a renowned Australian martial artist and weapons expert who co-starred with me in *The Octagon* and is now a film star himself, told me that he was training with the Machados, jujitsu instructors in Redondo Beach, California. Richard was so enthusiastic about them that I went along with him to their *dojo*, the name given to any place where karate, judo, aikido, and other Japanese martial arts are practiced.

It turned out that the Machados were all descendants of Carlos Gracie Sr. Theirs was quite a family: The instructors were Carlos Machado and his younger brothers, John, Rigan, and Jean-Jacques. That meeting was to be the first of many training sessions with Carlos and his brothers, a close-knit family, remarkably humble about their expertise. In my opinion, they are among the foremost jujitsu practitioners in the world today.

One day recently, after training with Carlos, we sat on the mat sipping bottled water and talked about the theory of jujitsu. "Our goal," he said, "is to neutralize aggression to achieve harmony. But you can only do that if you lose your ego. The egotistic person has not achieved harmony with himself or anyone else for that matter because he must try to convince everyone he is the best, which would be apparent were it true. A right-minded person is open to new ideas and approaches."

Our conversation was interrupted by a man who appeared to be angry and impatient. Carlos explained that it was his landlord, and excused himself. As the minutes passed, I saw the landlord beginning to relax and his voice become quieter. When he finally left he was smiling and cordially shook hands with Carlos.

I asked Carlos what had been going on.

"You and I have talked about how we can apply the Zen philosophy to our lives, and this is a case in point. My landlord came here determined to raise the rent. He began the discussion with me by anticipating a confrontation, which didn't occur. As you well know, that initial element of surprise is the basic premise of jujitsu. When you are attacked, you give way just enough to unbalance your opponent, and then turn the attack to your advantage by using skill or strategy.

"Most people fear an attack by somebody bigger or stronger than they are, but if you allow yourself to be intimidated and fearful, then your opponent has gained even more power.

But if your attitude is that no matter how strong or powerful the attacker is — and in this case my landlord was convinced he had the upper hand — you are better prepared, because you have trained and you have knowledge he does not possess, at that point he's vulnerable.

"So I waited for the landlord to complete his attack, and then I used each of his arguments against him. I told him that I was unable to pay an increase in rent, and suggested that in today's business climate he might not find another tenant so easily. If he did, he would probably have to paint and redecorate, and the place would probably be empty for several months. I also reminded him of the high bankruptcy rate for new businesses: The new tenant might move out quickly. I pointed out that for three years I had always paid the rent on time. I had added improvements, and I never asked him to help out with costly repairs such as plumbing, although I could legally have done so.

"When I had him off-balance, I brought him down with a surprise move. I had done some research and learned that recent laws had been passed that require new tenants to have a certain number of parking spaces for each five hundred square feet they occupy. There are no parking spaces available for the building. Since I have been here such a long time, I don't come under that law, but a new tenant would.

"My research into the new law was the move that took him off balance and sent him out of here thinking he was lucky to have me remain and deciding not to ask for an increase in rent."

What I have learned from my own study of jujitsu is that in most confrontations, in business as well as on the street, there are many elements involved, some of which can be used to your advantage, and those elements that you control can often mean the difference between winning and losing. The skilled master of life never tries to change things by asserting himself against them; he yields to their full force and either pushes them slightly out of direct line or else transfers their energy so that it can be used against them. He accepts life positively, and when events must be changed, he negotiates rather than inflicting his will on others.

BECOMING YOURSELF

He who conquers himself is the mightiest warrior.

— *Confucius*

The area in Korea where I trained for my black belt in karate was just a stretch of hard ground enclosed by bamboo fencing. When it was too cold or the rain was serious enough, we moved inside and did our workouts in a Quonset hut, but most of the time we were outside on that hard ground. I took my first steps toward becoming myself under that Korean sky, within those bamboo walls, which we called a *dojang,* the Korean word for dojo.

The name *dojo* was borrowed from the Buddhist nomenclature for the halls set aside for meditation and other spiritual exercises in virtually every monastery and convent, and the original Sanskrit word, *bodhimandala,* means "the place of enlightenment." Even when located far from a temple, the atmosphere of a proper dojo, where martial arts are taught in the traditional manner, reflects that historical background. It's a good name, short but with a deep meaning, and it says a lot about what really goes on in the practice of martial arts.

The primary elements of a dojo's atmosphere are the basic elements involved in learning any martial art: respect and discipline. Respect begins the first time a martial arts student steps into a dojo and bows to his instructor, often called a *sensei,* who in effect has the position of supreme authority and unchallenged prestige. Far from being a quaint holdover of Oriental tradition, the bows performed in a dojo are an outward expression of respect for someone in authority, regardless of age.

The bow is a formality, of course, and some American students rankle at it — they want to hurry along and learn how to do back kicks or perform karate or judo "chops." Such students usually need to give more thought to why they're in the dojo and what they hope to accomplish there.

Discipline is absolutely demanded by each martial art: You cannot advance without achieving certain goals, and you cannot hope to achieve the goals without adhering to a special set of rules. The rules, too, sometimes go against the grain of American students, but far from standing in the way of what is being taught, the rules mark off the only path to truly understanding a martial art.

The rules and discipline serve another purpose by turning away all but the truly dedicated. They're like the waiting period that aspiring monks must spend outside the door of a Zen temple; they're tests of resolve. Having agreed to abide by the rules, having agreed to accept — perhaps for the first time in their lives — what they cannot immediately understand, the students can begin learning a martial art in a dojo.

Discipline does not always have to be harsh, however:

When I started to learn a martial art in Korea, there were many days when I really didn't feel like working out: I was tired or bruised, often discouraged because I didn't seem to be improving, which caused me to be embarrassed when I was on the mat. My instructor recognized my problems and gently encouraged me with small praise or helpful hints on how I might improve. He was instilling discipline, not with the rod, but with gentle affection. Thanks to his teaching and discipline I went on to get my black belt and feel better about myself with a yearning to taste that feeling of accomplishment again.

In a very real sense the relationship with the instructor, or sensei, closely resembles the link between a stern father and a submissive son who is totally obedient to authority. This relationship is an integral part of the student-teacher bond because the teacher is the sole source of authority and knowledge and is entitled to respect because he or she has earned it. It's difficult for many American youths to accept this kind of ultimate authority — especially in the school room — but with time most students do come to realize that that's the way it is and must be for the student to learn.

People study martial arts for many reasons, sometimes all the wrong reasons. For example, I have had potential students come to my dojo with a belligerent and cocky attitude. When I ask why they want to study my art, their response has indicated to me that their goal is to learn to fight, which is the antithesis of the philosophy I hope to instill: I want them to know how to defend themselves if necessary, but to avoid fighting whenever possible because they will have nothing to prove by fighting. (The basic philosophy of all martial arts, a direct association with Zen, is not winning. In point of fact, most of the arts are designed to skillfully control conflict and win-lose situations.)

Of course, you can practice a martial art just about anywhere, and I've worked out and given lessons in backyards
and driveways, living rooms and hotel hallways. I suppose
such places could be called dojos, but usually the time spent
is too brief, the lessons involve only questions of technique,
and they begin and end informally, more like an entertaining
diversion than a movement toward some inner goal.

The basic philosophy of any martial art is designed to bring
you closer to yourself. That's what the dojo is for: to help the
student find the way to personal enlightenment. What goes
on in a real dojo requires more than physical movement; it
also demands mental concentration combined with a special
openness. You are there to learn, and much of that learning involves discoveries that come from inside. Put simply,
you can't perform a martial art if you're worried about your
marriage, school work, or about some big business deal. You
can't learn because you won't be listening to your instructor,
and you can't compete because your opponent will see that
gap in your concentration as clearly as he would spot a drop
in your defenses. You can't hope to find yourself, because
your vision is blocked by a thousand seemingly all-important
details.

When you step into the dojo, or even as you put on your *gi*
(martial art uniform) before beginning a workout, you have
to leave all those concerns behind. Some people feel out of
place and awkward during their first lessons — even during
the first few months of lessons. They arrive at the dojo seeing
themselves in a certain way — whether as director of public
affairs, mail room clerk, or housewife — and they lose energy
and control by trying to reinvent themselves in order to be a
person who can bow to their instructor and wear their gi. The
atmosphere of the dojo seems alien, the gi feels funny, and they

themselves feel awkward and embarrassed. But eventually, if they stick with it and learn the respect and discipline necessary, they begin to feel more at ease in the dojo, more like themselves — but different selves, without their usual clothes and without their official titles.

In the dojo, the director, clerk, and housewife are equal in an absolute sense, dressed alike, treated the same way by the instructor, striving together and alone for the same goals. Thus in the dojo they become what seems to be another person, someone who wears much less clothing and is routinely asked to perform difficult — sometimes seemingly impossible — acts with their bodies. That ability to leave the day-to-day concerns behind with their street clothes is the first major step toward a kind of enlightenment; eventually it is the same person who wears the gi and the business suit, and that person is calmer and more sure of himself or herself, that person has a new inner strength. In one place, the dojo, it means having the control to see an opponent setting up for a kick and instantly moving to avoid or block it; in another place — whether the boardroom or bedroom — it means listening with an open and calm mind and knowing and behaving in a controlled and responsible way.

Had I not discovered martial arts when I was in the service, I probably would have returned home and taken the first job that was offered to me because I had a wife and child to support. I had only a high school education and was insecure in my ability to succeed in an environment where a higher education was required. Martial arts changed my life by giving me a sense of accomplishment, a sense of discipline, but even more, a good sense of myself. Martial arts can be likened to sports, but the playing field is far larger, and the goal is something beyond just winning. If you are successful in your training, you'll find yourself on the road to understanding why the dojo is the "place of enlightenment."

Conquering yourself is a slow, often arduous, process, but it can be done by maintaining discipline and respect for yourself and others.

STAY WITH
THE MOMENT

For the uncontrolled there is no wisdom, nor for the
uncontrolled is there the power of concentration.

— *Bhagavad Gita*

After I earned my black belt in Korea, finally reaching a goal
I had worked more than a year to achieve, I began to slacken
up a bit in practice sessions, sometimes going through the mo-
tions mechanically as my mind wandered between thoughts
of the future and of my wife back home alone in the States,
waiting for my return.

I thought Mr. Jae Chul Shin, my sensei, would not notice.
After all, I was making the right movements, performing each
exercise in the prescribed manner. And I was but one student
of many on the mat working out. But Mr. Shin saw immediately. He let me get away with this for a while — perhaps it
was his way of giving me a rest after my effort for the black
belt — but then after one session he took me aside.

"Your mind is not here," he said. I made no effort to deny that he was right; students of martial arts soon learn that their teachers can see right through them. Standing there on the hard ground of the workout area in Korea, I just bowed my head slightly and waited for Mr. Shin to continue.

"What you are doing at the moment must be *exactly* what you are doing at the moment — and nothing else," he said. "There is no control when the mind is absent. You must be one with yourself and with what you are doing. While doing something, you are doing it at the fullest. That is true Zen."

"What is Zen?" I asked. It was the first time I had heard the word, and, because Mr. Shin's English was so difficult to understand, I did not know what he meant until years later.

"It is the basic thing," he said.

"But I don't remember your teaching it to me."

"I didn't, but you will learn it," he said somewhat enigmatically.

Although puzzled, I resolved to concentrate totally on what I was doing during the next workout, and I did. I had no thoughts of anything else, and when the session ended, Mr. Shin bowed, smiled, and said, "Ah, you are learning Zen."

Zen lessons are not about cause and effect. They're about learning what you knew all along; about learning by forgetting what you thought you had learned. I'd had my first Zen lesson without even knowing it.

When I was discharged and I returned home to Los Angeles from Korea I began to enter karate tournaments. Often I would have to drive for hours, even days, to the tournament. By the time I arrived, my mind would be racing, concerned with issues that had no relationship to the matter at hand: Should I wait until before or after the match to eat? Did I have money enough to stay in a motel or should I plan to sleep in the car? What were my wife and infant son doing? Would my old car make it home?

Before I stepped into the ring I could hear the spectators cheering and calling out names, and I'd listen for my own. I was aware of the temperature in the arena. There were a hundred distractions, large and small: teammates giving last-minute suggestions, and my own mind, running over plans for the fight one last time.

No one, not even a lover, looks at you as intensely and closely as someone who intends to knock you out in the ring. I could actually feel my opponent's eyes drilling into me, examining my slightest movement, measuring my breathing, calculating my physical condition. And I did the same to him. It's no exaggeration to say that winning or losing a bout is directly related to concentration. A gap in your concentration is a hole in your defense — and your competitor will spot it immediately and make his move. Mr. Shin's advice, my first lesson in Zen, came back to me again and again during my years as a competitor: What you are doing at the moment must be *exactly* what you are doing at the moment — and nothing else.

Applying this particular lesson to everyday life can sometimes seem nigh unto impossible, but it can be done. Living in the present without permitting thoughts of the past or concerns for the future to intrude requires a special kind of concentration and focus. Most of all, it means slowing down and opening up. It means being truly open to other people, listening to all of what they are saying instead of trying to reduce their concerns to a problem that can be briskly solved. It means seeing what is really in front of you without permitting other concerns to block or cloud your vision. There's a popular saying about taking the time to smell the roses. It may not have the ring of a Zen aphorism — somehow it's hard to imagine roses growing near a Zen monastery — but, like so many old sayings, it's based on a truism of life. We walk by rose bushes, sometimes even entire gardens of those flowers, and we're aware in passing that they're beautiful; maybe we even take the time to say so: "Pretty flowers." What the saying wants us to do is take even more time, enough to stand still and actually smell them. In a sense, it means we should take the time to see and understand what the roses really are, for without their smell they'd be something else.

Even now, while doing other things, my mind will sometimes suddenly tear itself loose to dream, to fancy, to race aimlessly like a hamster in a cage, to hold internal conversations — anything to avoid the reality of the present. Often there are people around me requiring attention and offering suggestions, making it difficult for me to create order out of chaos. At those times I again fall back on Mr. Shin's advice and force myself to concentrate on one problem at a time, excluding all other thoughts from my mind.

I have found that to be here and not anywhere else is the key to total concentration. By living in the present, I am in full contact with myself and my environment; my energy is not dissipated and is always available. In the present there are no regrets, as there must be when thinking of the past, and worrying about the future only dilutes our awareness of the present. I have learned to focus all of my concentration on each individual moment, whether it's a voice on the other end of a phone line, a face looking at me from across a desk, that single eye of a camera, or that rose garden. There is only now, only this moment. There is nothing else. Nothing.

JUST DO IT

The emperor Butei sent for the Zen master Fu-daishi to have him explain the *Diamond Sutra,* an explanation of Zen doctrines based on aphorisms derived from ancient sages. On the appointed day Fu-daishi came to the palace, mounted a platform, rapped the table before him, then descended and, still without speaking a word, left.

The emperor sat motionless, looking up at the empty platform. Then Shiko, a Zen disciple who had seen all that had happened, went up to him and said, "May I be so bold, sir, as to ask whether you understood?"

The emperor sadly shook his head.

"What a pity!" Shiko exclaimed. "Fu-daishi has never been more eloquent!"

One of the basic tenets of Zen is that it really has nothing at all to teach, nothing at all to say: According to Zen, the truth is obvious, or should be. The truth is nothing that can be taught.

You can't sit down at a desk and wait for a lecturer to step up to the podium and reveal the truth to you. Instead, you have to become aware of it on your own.

The "silence" of Zen hasn't kept people from writing entire libraries on the subject, books that explore what goes on between Zen masters and their students. This accumulated Zen "teaching" often seems abstruse, even outlandishly strange.

Zen is the peculiarly Chinese way of seeing the world just as it is; that is, with a mind that has no grasping thoughts or feelings. This attitude is called "no mind," a state of consciousness wherein thoughts move without leaving any trace. Zen practitioners believe that such freedom of mind cannot be attained by gradual practice but must come through direct and immediate insight, what I think of as intuition.

There are no logical steps to intuition: Either you see the truth at once or you don't see it at all. This "sudden enlightenment," which the Japanese call *satori,* is a basic element of Zen and one of its major appeals.

Too many times in my life I have approached a situation with my mind cluttered with concerns about the outcome. My mind was blocked instead of being open. My reactions were either predetermined or influenced by contrary thoughts, and therefore I was likely to miss important signals or clues that could have been helpful. I had hindered my ability to intuit.

Over the years I have let intuition — one might call it "gut reaction" — take over, and my responses have usually been correct. In a purely Zen sense, action is better than inaction, and the decision to move awakens the powers of intuition that will find the right path.

The enormous importance of Zen to martial arts practitioners is clear: The intuition of Zen eliminates mental "blocking," and this elimination of blocking can be applied equally to mental as well as physical action, freeing the martial artist to move and respond fluidly, on the basis of intuition and without reflection.

Those who dedicate themselves openly and fully to an art, be it painting, writing poetry, gardening, architecture, calligraphy, preparing tea, or any other creative process, eventually find themselves moving toward Zen. Zen brings an appreciation and understanding of the simplest aspects, the most mundane gestures, involved in the art, and Zen frees the artist to move with the flow of the art rather than blocking all creativity with overwrought plans or preconceived notions. Zen even leads to a kind of delight in "mistakes": what might seem out of place to others may actually reveal itself to the Zen artist as a fortuitous indication of the right direction.

In a sense, the martial artist moves toward Zen along the same route as the Zen disciple, who must reason out complicated problems under the guidance of a master who moves him forward indirectly, by misleading him and thus forcing him to find the way himself. The martial artist studies the complicated physical movements known as *heians,* and his teacher places different "blocks" in his path, always demanding further effort, asking him over and over to do the impossible. And when the student has done that, he asks for it again but in a new form.

Both the Zen monk, constantly forced to ponder questions that seem impossible, and the martial artist, required each day to move and react with increasingly complicated movements, are examples of the Zen use of repetition. This repetition is a form of exercise designed to create intuition, to make the mind or body able to flow without reflection or pause. This "doing it" over and over eventually reveals what could be called the "Zen" of the action, an understanding that goes beyond meaning or purpose and awards the practitioner with a unique sense of being at one with his or her activity. A difficult process, it can, and often does, lead to frustration. Martial arts students eventually find themselves asking the same question of their master: How can they perfect what seems to them to be already perfect? How can they move with any more accuracy when they are already hitting the center? And in response, ever and always, they find themselves being told only to hit the center once again. The day comes when they understand the reasons behind the repetitions, and on that day they look on their master with renewed respect.

I've seen this aspect of Zen applied to guidance for getting ahead in business, based on the theory, I suppose, that it's a cutthroat world and you need to be as well trained as a samurai to have any hope of survival. Most often, this concept is translated as "simply being prepared," "doing your homework." I'd take it even farther and include it as one of the first entries on any list of sensible things to do to maximize your chance of success in any field of endeavor: Don't spread yourself thin. Determine to know more about your field than anyone else, and make what you know your own: Visualize everything you learn — imagine yourself actually applying the lessons.

And, most important of all, the aspect that is all too often forgotten: *Do it*. Then do it again, and when you think you've learned it all, do it all again from a slightly different angle. It's a wonderful thing to see a professional athlete perform what he or she does best. Their skill always makes it look so easy. It's obvious that their minds are clear and uncluttered with worries about, "Can I do it?" They already know they can. They've done it a thousand times before, so they do it.

WINNING BY LOSING

What goes on in the ring during a martial arts tournament may seem like raw violence — sudden, unpredictable moves, leaps and kicks, deft blocks and punches. The truth is that every move the two contestants make is controlled, carefully monitored by several referees, sometimes as many as five. The participants have spent long hours preparing for their few moments in the ring, and the moves they make with lightning speed are not random, but are based on hard-learned lessons and exhausting practice. There are always surprises, because everyone's always attempting to use a new move to throw opponents off-balance, but what happens follows certain rules. The winner wins and the loser loses because of precise measurements and decisions.

The truth is that the competitors in the ring aren't enemies, but friends — not just because they all know one another and really are good friends off the mat, but because they're working together to achieve something. The bout itself is a kind of group effort at achieving something, and if it's carried off properly, the winner will have won more than his name on a trophy, and the loser will go away with an important lesson for tomorrow: He will never lose that way again.

Those lessons — the ones that come from losing — are invaluable. Nothing can ever point out the existence of a hole in a defense so clearly as seeing an opponent penetrate it; nothing can indicate a problem with timing like throwing a kick and encountering only air.

Back when I was competing in the ring, one of my primary rules for myself was that I would never lose the same way twice. "Learn from your mistakes" is an old rule, but it's surprising how many people fail to heed it. It means recognizing that the loss resulted from something you did wrong. It wasn't because the referees or judges were blind, or that the mat was slippery, or because they've changed all the rules around. Excuses like these do nothing more than place an artificial bandage on wounded dignity; if you can't see the lesson in what went wrong, you're just condemning yourself to making the same mistake again.

So you work out harder, you talk to other people and learn what they have to teach you, and you practice — there's no excuse for not doing your homework, for not being prepared.

Of course, you can lose even if you're in the best physical shape possible. And that brings up the most important aspect of all this, an aspect that is both simple and obvious — and is thus what some people would call Zen. Past a certain point, once you've mastered your art and brought yourself up to the peak of perfection, chances are that each time you lose it's a result of the same problem: your mind.

During a tournament in 1967 I lined up for the matches and found myself standing next to a young student who had just earned his black belt. At the time, I was rated number one in the country, a fact he was very much aware of. The poor kid was so nervous about fighting me that he had to rush out to the bathroom before the match. Seeing him suffer like that made me feel sorry for him. I put my arm around him and told him not to worry.

He beat me, of course. My number one ranking meant nothing at all if my mind was out of control. My feeling sorry for him was a form of overconfidence: I eased up, and he was good enough to spot his chance and grab it.

Anger is the best example. I've seen scores of matches won or lost as a result of one participant getting angry, easily the surest way to lose control and cloud your mind. I used it against Skipper Mullins once in the Internationals. We were in the last round of our match, and he was ahead on points, so he was avoiding me, running out of the ring, to run out the time.

I said to him, "Why don't you stay in the ring and fight like a man?" It worked; he got angry, came back at me, and I beat him. For years I have kidded him about losing his cool, and as a result, losing the match.

Anger, the desire to inflict defeat on an opponent because of some real or imagined wrong, has no place in a martial arts match. To outsiders it might seem paradoxical, but the "fighting" of martial arts competitions usually — ideally — involves no anger.

No anger, pride, or overconfidence — nothing that will blur your vision or cloud your mind — belongs in the ring. Lack of emotional control can also turn an otherwise ordinary day into a day you'll regret: The control you learn on the mat will serve you well off it. You can't win in a tournament if you lose your mental control, and pretty much the same thing can be said for the rest of life. If you control yourself and your behavior, other people will treat you with respect, eliminating any reason for conflict.

⌣

Not long ago after a hard day of filming my television series, I went alone to a small Texas bar for a cold beer. I was dressed in character for my role, scruffy and dirty from doing a fight scene in the dirt. I sat in a corner booth enjoying the country Western music and savoring my drink. A man large enough to cast a shadow over the table towered over me and said I was sitting in his booth. He suggested with an edge to his voice that I vacate to make room for him and his friends.

I didn't like the tone of his voice or the threat implicit in his suggestion if I failed to heed it, but I said nothing and got up and moved to another booth. A few minutes later some of the stuntmen from the show arrived and joined me.

I noticed the big fellow eyeing me and saw him get up and head for our table. Here it comes, I thought, a local tough out to make a name for himself by taking on Chuck Norris in a fight.

When he arrived at our booth, he ignored the others and looked directly at me. "You're Chuck Norris," he said.

I nodded.

"Hey, man," he said. "You could have whipped my ass back there a few minutes ago. Why didn't you?"

"What would it have proved?" I said.

He thought that over for a moment and then smiled and offered me his hand. "No hard feelings?" he said.

"None," I said and shook his hand.

I had avoided a confrontation and made a friend. I won by losing.

I recall a story told to me by a martial artist friend. He was at a stop sign waiting for a break in traffic that would allow him to cross a major street safely. The driver in the car behind him impatiently honked his horn. Finally losing patience, the driver got out and began to threaten my friend if he didn't find the gas pedal.

My friend rolled down the driver's window and said, "You want to fight. Okay, but I have a bad back, and you will have to help me out of the car."

The man looked at my friend, shook his head wonderingly, and returned to his car.

Luckily for the impatient driver, the situation had been defused by humor. He had no idea how close he had come to being thrashed.

SUCCESS IS IN YOUR
MIND'S EYE

During the years I taught, I guided more than 325 students to black belt status. Although all of them had to meet the same demanding standards and pass the same test, no two students were alike, and for each of them the road to passing that final test was different, if only because each began the journey from a different background, a different place in life. All of them had hurdles to get over, whether physical, mental, or emotional. The hurdle usually appeared early on — a flawed mental attitude or some perceived physical failing — but sometimes the hurdle made its appearance only near the end.

I had one student, a natural athlete if ever there was one. His technique was flawless, just about right from the start. His every movement was perfectly synchronized, his posture was proud, and in practice sessions he easily defeated students with much more training. He learned easily and quickly, and I was certain he had the potential to be one of the best students

I had ever had. He wanted me to promote him to a higher rank before he was eligible because he was defeating higher-ranked students. I explained that martial arts are more than just physical ability, a higher rank demanded more growth of maturity than he had achieved. He couldn't understand that there was more to martial arts than winning a bout, so he quit. That distressed me, because I knew he would never realize his potential.

I can't help but contrast him with another student, one who was probably the least athletic man I had ever taught. He had only one thing going for him — determination. I found myself full of apprehension when he became eligible to test for his black belt, for I was sure he wouldn't pass. He didn't. Afterward, I took him aside and explained to him point by point why he had failed the test.

"Fine," he said. "I'll work on the areas where I'm weak." And he did work. But when the time came, he again failed the black belt test. I again reviewed his problems with him, and he again worked to improve, but he failed the test three more times. He was clumsy and awkward, his mind seemingly elsewhere rather than on what he had trained to do.

After the test I found him sitting alone on a bench staring disconsolately into space. He barely looked up when I approached and said only, "I blew it again. I couldn't think. I couldn't move. I was tight all over my body." He asked me if I thought he could ever pass the test.

"How badly do you want to pass?" I asked him.

"More than anything else in the world," he said.

I put my hand on his shoulder and said, "Then you will make it. Sometimes, when the pressure's on, your mind and body tense up because you're nervous. You become mentally and physically inhibited, and you choke. But it happens to everyone from Olympic athletes to school kids at exam time. It's nothing to be ashamed of."

"Did it ever happen to you?" he asked.

I told him of the time I took my first black belt test in Seoul, Korea, after a year of almost daily practice to the point of exhaustion. It was in the dead of winter and bitterly cold. My sergeant let me borrow a truck from the car pool for the forty-five-mile drive. When I arrived at the dojo after two hours of driving on icy roads, I was stiff with cold, and it was -8 degrees inside as well as outside the training hall. I was so keyed up by thinking about the test that my brain felt like it was going to explode.

I was the only one from my school among two hundred strangers, all Koreans, there to test for various ranks. I watched them with interest for half an hour, but soon my mind could focus only on how stiff and cold I was. After about three hours of sitting with body and mind numb with cold, I heard my name called.

I went before the examiners, bowed, and was told to do a heian, a form I had done to perfection countless times before. But on this day I choked. I told the examiners I couldn't remember the heian. I was ordered back to my place and had to wait several more hours until the others finished testing before I could leave.

I was miserable on the long drive alone back to the base, and ashamed to face Mr. Shin, my instructor. He never mentioned my failure and left me alone to train for another three months. I put the first exam out of my mind; I knew that if I spent time dwelling on my failure, I would put failure in my subconscious. Instead, I thought only of success and imagined myself performing each movement with perfection. I studied the black belts in my class carefully. If I had no success of my own to draw on, I would draw success from theirs, and I visualized myself in their place doing what they did. I *stole* their behavior, made it mine in my mind's eye and inside my body.

I realized that it was not the test that was important; it was what I made of it. I mentally rehearsed the test over and over, visualizing myself doing every movement perfectly, creating an image of success in my mind. I knew the goal and I knew how to reach it. There was no way I was going to crash and burn again: I had everything I was expected to do memorized and grooved in my mind so that even under pressure I would re-act automatically. The next time I took the test I passed it as I knew I would.

"Choking happens when you let pressure control you rather than controlling the pressure yourself. A normal response to pressure is self-defeating, because under pressure the heart speeds up and triggers nervousness," I told my student. "Always remember that your success begins inside you: If you can't see it first, no one else ever will."

The student passed his test six months later. When I presented him with his new black belt, he smiled.

"You were right," he told me. "When it was my turn to go on the mat, I started to choke again, and then I visualized myself doing everything perfectly as I had practiced. I knew I could do it, and I did."

GET OUT OF YOUR
OWN WAY

The last time I saw my father he was standing alone in front of a bar in Wilson, Oklahoma, looking old and worn out. This was back in the summer of 1962, and I hadn't seen or heard from him for several years. I'd just got my discharge from the air force, and there was a lot I could have told him about myself and my life, but in the end all I said was that I was married and that my wife was expecting — pretty much the kind of news you'd swap with a barber or a stranger sitting next to you on an airplane.

"Great," he said, and walked back into the bar. And that was that.

My father was a perfect example of someone who never takes control of his life. The sad truth is that he just drifted through his life, stumbling over himself, offering excuses whenever he failed, and refusing to accept responsibility for his actions.

A lot of people are like my father was, just sort of wandering along, getting by from day to day. It isn't that they don't have dreams, visions of themselves achieving some great success; it's that along with those dreams they also have a host of excuses based on rock-solid arguments that block their path in an instant whenever they think that maybe, just maybe, the day has come to do something about those dreams. Something always comes along to get in their way. It's the wrong time of year, or their car's in the shop, or they're too tired after whatever it was they did last night. That's what they say, but the truth is that the only thing in their way is themselves.

I'm reminded of a phrase a student of mine used several years ago. Just a beginner, he was having trouble with his timing. When he moved his legs and arms at the same time but in different directions, he tripped himself up, half the time landing flat out on his back on the mat. Once, after he'd done just that, he looked up at me from the mat and said, full of frustration, "I keep getting in my own way."

His problem was relatively easy to solve, in large part because of his attitude. He knew he was doing something wrong and was eager to learn the right way, was open to everything I said. For him, it was really just a matter of learning each movement individually and then combining them, fitting them together to make them flow; but a lot of people get in their own way in a far more difficult sense. They prevent themselves from succeeding by creating their own obstacles, by tripping themselves up without any interference at all from the outside world.

There's a famous Zen koan about the proper way of greeting a stranger encountered on the path of life. You can think about the question in several ways, but to me, the most valid one is that the stranger you meet is meant to be yourself: How will you greet yourself? How will you judge yourself as you go about your life? You can visualize the koan as two figures, you and the stranger, standing face-to-face on a path, and looked at that way, you can see a kind of paradox: Nothing blocks the stranger's forward movement along the path except you standing there, and, in the same way, nothing blocks your forward movement, nothing at all restricts you except yourself, for you are the stranger.

That's a fact that's hard to accept, even harder to live by. You can usually see your way around the blocks that other people put in your path, but the blocks you create yourself, the ones that come from inside your own thinking, seem rooted in the ground and as wide as the horizon. As indeed they are, for you yourself are standing in the way.

The way around the block is from the inside; from the Zen point of view, the only place the block has reality is inside yourself. If you're being less successful than you had hoped or expected, don't make excuses and don't look around for some stranger to blame. Instead, check the three components of a winning attitude: mental toughness, psychological preparedness, and physical condition. An uncorrected deficiency in any of these areas will drag the other two down. Being in great physical shape won't get you far if you're full of doubts about your abilities, if you're always comparing yourself to others and finding yourself lacking, or if you're foolishly overconfident. In the same way, no matter how carefully you plan or how clearly you can visualize your ultimate success, it won't come to much if you don't dedicate your time and effort to working out, to keeping yourself physically alert and capable, to doing your homework. Remember, too, that you believe the thoughts you send yourself, your subconscious thoughts, more than the words of others, so make those thoughts positive, one at a time, and then make them move together in time with your life. If you learn to think positively, your subconscious will go along, even working for you while you sleep. You sleep; it doesn't. In time, all the blocks will disappear, and the path ahead will be clear.

Learn to think kindly of yourself, to pay yourself the respect you'd pay someone else. Learn to greet yourself the way you'd greet a stranger — politely, open to the possibility that you might be about to make a friend for life, aware that the person standing in front of you could be anyone, could come from anywhere, could be about to accomplish anything. The stranger could be about to make any number of dreams come true. And having greeted the stranger, realize that all those things are equally true of yourself, standing on the path of life. At any given time or any given place, you may be about to accomplish the dream of a lifetime — yours — but only if you open yourself up.

I am reminded of a day in 1968 when I was at the airport on my way to San Francisco to give a karate demonstration. I had brought a book with me to read on the flight and was waiting to check in when I saw one of my students in the line with a friend of his. I hoped they wouldn't notice me because I wanted to read, not talk. As luck would have it, my student saw me and asked me to join him and his friend on the plane. At first I thought, "No way," but my intuition was to sit with them. Unbeknownst to me, that was to be a turning point in my life, because I met Larry Morales, who was to become one of my best friends and the man who would be responsible for helping me get started in films.

The moral of my story: You never know when a meeting with a stranger may change the course of your life if you get out of your own way.

CONTROL YOUR
EMOTIONS

I first became aware of the current kick boxing champion, Benny "the Jet" Urquidez, in 1965, when I was competing in the Internationals in Long Beach, California, the largest karate tournament in the world, with more than three thousand fighters entered. One of my opponents in the middleweight division was Benny's older brother, Arnold Urquidez, who was a good friend. While we were waiting to be called up for matches, Arnold asked me if I would go with him to watch a young fighter who, he said, showed lots of promise.

To my surprise, Arnold led me to a mat on the far side of the stadium, where some white belts in the junior class were sparring. "That one," said Arnold, pointing to a tow-headed kid of about twelve, who was easily trouncing his opponent with a combination of techniques far superior to any I had seen performed by a youngster of that age. Equally important, I admired the boy's spunk. It's not that he was fearless, he just wasn't afraid of getting hurt.

"That's my kid brother, Benny," Arnold proudly said. "What do you think?"

"He's tremendously talented," I said.

I wasn't surprised, however. I knew that Arnold's father had been a pro boxer, and his mother had been a pro wrestler. His other brothers, Ruben and Smiley (Adam), and his sister Lilly were all into karate.

As we walked to the other side of the stadium, Arnold told me that Benny had grown up in a gym since the age of three. "While other kids wanted fire trucks, Benny wanted boxing gloves. He was boxing in the peewee class at the age of five."

Later that day, I noticed little Benny watching the black belts sparring and trying to imitate their moves.

In time Benny came to be something of a mascot to Arnold and me. Whenever Arnold and I went to the church in Little Tokyo where we sometimes worked out with Bruce Lee, Benny always asked to come along. He sat quietly, watching and absorbing everything that he saw.

When he was eleven years old, Benny had a brown belt in *kenpo-shotokan,* Arnold's style. At the age of fourteen, he was a handful for many of the more advanced black belts. At that time there was a tradition that a *karateka* had to be eighteen years old to test for his black belt. Although Benny was only five feet two inches tall and barely broke a hundred pounds, he was so advanced that Ed Parker and some other black belts decided to break the rules and allow him to test for his black belt. Arnold, a real traditionalist, was opposed to the test, but he went along with the majority.

Benny passed his test easily. Tradition then called for all the black belts to line up one at a time and take turns aiming kicks at the new *shodan* (first-degree black belt) who was supposed to take their force without yielding or complaining.

Arnold kicked his little brother so hard that he broke three of Benny's ribs.

When Benny turned eighteen, Ed Parker hired him to tour the country teaching black belt instructors in his chain of schools, Benny's first job outside of the family dojo.

Benny now has a black belt in nine different styles and has taken the best from each style and made it work under pressure. He learned to speedily close the distance between himself and an opponent by studying shotokan karate; his side step was developed by studying white crane kung fu; to speed up his kicks he studied tae kwon do; to develop more power in his kicks and better use of his elbows and knees he studied muay thai. Benny perfected his ground grappling ability by learning aikido, judo and jujitsu, under the guidance of Gene LeBell.

During his years of activity in the ring, Benny always dominated his weight division and became the World Champion in every sanctioning body under which he fought: undefeated in nineteen years, his official ring record is 58–0 with forty-nine knockouts. He won most of his bouts in the days when full-contact karate was in vogue. Contestants had tape on their knuckles and two toes, and that was it for protection. Heads and noses were split open, but the contest went on. Fights didn't end on the ground; they ended when one fighter couldn't continue, and when it was over, the warriors embraced with genuine respect for each other.

For many years Benny, nicknamed "Benny the Jet," because of his ability to deliver a jump-spinning back kick, had his own Jet Center in Los Angeles, where fighters from all over the world came to train with him. Not interested in training them only physically, Benny was also dedicated to training them mentally.

Recently, at the age of forty-one, Benny, who hadn't fought in more than four years, agreed to a retirement fight. His opponent was the Japanese World Kick Boxing Champion, Yoshiba Tagami, a twenty-five-year-old pro with a 22–0 record and twelve knockouts.

The fight took place in Las Vegas in December 1993. I was there, too, offering color as a commentator. It was a heated battle, with both fighters taking and giving punishment in each round. Although no one was aware of it, Benny broke his left hand, his power hand, during the third round, but nevertheless, he continued to fight. The furious twelve-round battle ended with Benny the victor. Tagami, with tears in his eyes, bowed to Benny, a gesture of honor and respect rarely seen after championship bouts.

Later, many of Benny's friends and students went to his hotel, where we had a post-fight discussion. I recall someone asking Benny, who had been hurt and fouled several times, how he managed to control his anger. "You must be in control of all your emotions under pressure or you won't be relaxed and will lose your ability to respond easily and think clearly," Benny said. "If you get hurt and become angry and want to hurt in return, you won't think clearly and you won't be in control. If you're afraid, your concentration will be on avoiding getting hurt and not on the problem at hand. If you're frustrated, you will lose control."

Benny was absolutely right. From my own experience, I have come to believe that the body changes when under pressure: Reaction time quickens, you have greater strength, you move faster, your sense of pain is diminished, and you tend to get tunnel vision.

Under pressure you need to slow down, control your thoughts, and control your movements. I teach my students that they will get their control from practice, so much repetition of the proper moves that they become automatic.

On the mat their mental attitude must be what is known as the state of *muga,* that is, an absence of feeling that "I am doing it." Their concentration must be on the task at hand, and they must follow the opponent's movements so closely and respond to them so immediately that there is no time lag between attack and defense.

In life as well as on the mat, you have to recognize that in certain circumstances, such as a confrontation, your body and mind will switch to exaggerated behavior, so you have to adjust to those changes by taking your time and staying focused. You control your thoughts by concentrating on what's at hand, what really is the issue, not on what you imagine to be the issue. You have to know yourself and how you personally react when the heat is turned up, and believe you can manage it. You must maintain focus on the here and now, and then you are in control. The bottom line is you must believe in yourself.

There is, however, in my view, one more important element to controlling your emotions. Under pressure, most people start to breathe more heavily, and their bodies become tense. Zen practitioners in such circumstances gain control of their breathing, which in turn helps them relax.

One technique that I use is to imagine that during inhalation a very thin silver thread is drawn in uninterruptedly through the nostrils and flows down the spinal column, where it is held for a few seconds in the lower abdomen. Three-quarters of the air is then exhaled gently through the mouth in a steady, concentrated, powerful, but relaxed, stream — the sound of the exhalation resembling an "aah."

That simple breathing technique — a central part of Zen practice — is another key to controlling your emotions. As an actor-producer-writer of my own films and television series, I am often confronted with situations involving many people, some of them angry, belligerent, or defensive, and everyone looking to me for a solution to the problem.

In such situations, I find that controlled breathing restores calm, confidence, and strength. It also allows me to bring my emotions and thoughts under control so that I can concentrate on what's at hand.

Benny surprised a lot of people when he earned his black belt at fourteen, at an age when most young people quickly lose control, particularly when under great pressure. He surprised them even more when he successfully fought a man almost half his age decades later. I feel his ability to control his emotions was a major factor in his remarkable success. Today, he's an outstanding example of a martial artist who has achieved what can be called a Zen outlook by way of the discipline and experience of the martial arts. I have always told my students that they will find their best resources within themselves. Benny is proof of that.

SLOW DOWN
TO GO FASTER

I first met Bruce Lee in 1968 at Madison Square Garden, where I was fighting for the World Middleweight Karate Championships. I won, but not without taking a beating of my own. As I was leaving the stadium, Bruce came over to introduce himself and congratulate me. I knew of him, had seen him put on a terrific demonstration at the Long Beach Internationals a couple of years earlier, and I had also seen him on the *Green Hornet* television series.

We got to talking, found out we were staying in the same hotel, and kept each other company as we walked back together. It was nearly midnight when we arrived in the hotel, but neither of us made it to bed that night. Instead, we worked out together in a hallway of the hotel, exchanging techniques until seven the next morning. When we finally parted company, we agreed to get together again in Los Angeles, because our dedication to the martial arts was mutual. His drive was to learn, to get better within himself; my drive was similar but also to become a champion in order to get more students into my school.

During the next three years we met often, usually in the backyard of his house in Culver City or at my dojo, and shared ideas and techniques on a steady basis. We took turns as student and teacher, and through that exchange we became friends. Martial artists often trade fighting techniques and training tips, and neither Bruce nor I had any intention of being bound to any one style.

People who see Bruce only as a movie star miss the real man, for he was also an author and scholar: The walls of his living room and bedroom were lined with shelves of martial arts books, many of them in Chinese, and many of them about Zen. Bruce was always busy, appearing on television shows and teaching in his school in Los Angeles; but all the while, he was dedicated most of all to working out his personal philosophy. He was open to any new ideas, and that openness was contagious.

I learned various kung fu techniques from him, and I taught him high kicks, meaning kicks above the waist. The only formal martial arts training he'd had was under Yip Man, in Hong Kong, who'd taught him *wing chun,* a form of Chinese boxing that emphasized hand rather than foot techniques — most kicks were quick and delivered low, to the opponent's shin or knee. It didn't take long for me to convince Bruce that kicks could be effectively delivered to any area of the body, and he taught me many of the techniques of wing chun.

In those days, as now, my favorite technique was a spinning heel kick delivered with speed and force at my opponent, a skill I had learned in Korea and used to great advantage when I was competing in martial arts tournaments.

One day during a workout at Bruce's home, I scored on him constantly, despite his attempts to block my kicks. When we ended the workout he went into the house and came back carrying some oranges. We sat on the grass underneath a tree and peeled the oranges. I noticed that most of the bark was missing from one side of the tree and commented on that fact. Bruce laughed. "The tree is my target for kicks and punches," he said.

Bruce took off his T-shirt, and I marveled again as I always did every time I saw his physique; he had muscles on muscles.

As I sat and enjoyed the peace and quiet in the yard, Bruce counted off one-hand push-ups. After about fifty, he stopped and turned his attention to me. "No matter how much I tried I was unable to block your kicks," he said. "What am I doing wrong?"

"You tried to speed your blocks up," I said. "And your timing was off."

"Like when I practice sticky hands [a wing chun technique] with you. When you try to go faster, you score on me repeatedly."

"If I am getting better, it's because I've slowed down, and that's what I'm suggesting to you. Pace yourself, attend to everything in its own sweet time, and you'll accomplish more than if you go all out at every opportunity. Slow down and you'll go faster."

"That's a real Zen riddle," Bruce said: " 'Slow down to go faster.' I like it."

Bruce was right, of course, the concept does come from Zen, or at least reveals a Zen awareness. But I first came by it a long time ago, while working out alone, trying to get the awkwardness out of some new movements. When something is broken, you take it apart to fix it, and the same applies to the martial arts. When something isn't working, somehow isn't getting the results you hoped for or were told to expect, you break it down step by step to see if you can locate where it's going wrong. Breaking down a martial arts move means doing it slowly, and I found that by moving slowly, I could sense what was meant to be the inner balance of the move, each step serving its own specific purpose. Having sensed that inner balance and learned to adjust my body to it, and having discovered the importance of including each move, I found I could speed up the moves at will, performing them quickly or slowly with the same accuracy.

Since then I've come across the concept in other aspects of the martial arts, such as *bojutsu,* which is practiced by Japanese master swordsmen. Of all the ancient arts, that of sword fighting demands the greatest respect and attention, since its practitioners were well aware that their lives depended on their skills. They were also aware, however, that even the greatest mastery of technique could not guarantee their survival in combat, since it was always possible that the next opponent would be stronger or quicker.

The answer they found was a kind of slowing down. Rather than rush at an opponent, hoping to throw him off guard, they depended on instinct, a kind of inner detachment from both themselves and their opponent. Relying on it, they responded to each single thrust made by their opponent, breaking the combat down into its component parts and reacting as necessary to each one in order as it occurred, without ever trying to anticipate or force a move. Having mastered the ability to respond instinctively to any thrust, they could then move with lightning speed.

At first the notion of slowing down so he could go faster seemed contradictory to Bruce. But he did as I suggested and soon found that I was right. He forced himself to relax and then explode, and then relax again. His blocks and kicks improved.

Of course, there's a certain sadness attached to any story about Bruce Lee. In a sense, he was the James Dean of the martial arts world: a natural, a true star who died tragically young, at the age of thirty-two, as the result of a hypersensitive reaction to a headache-tablet ingredient.

I was in Los Angeles trying to get into a film when I learned of Bruce's death in Hong Kong. I had seen him only four days earlier in Los Angeles. He had come into town for a checkup because he had passed out while making a film in Hong Kong. We had dim sum in his favorite restaurant in Chinatown, and I still remember him tossing a piece of Peking duck into the air and catching it with his chopsticks, a neat feat for anyone, and then challenging me to do the same. I knew I couldn't do it, so I declined. Bruce told me that he'd passed the checkup with flying colors and was going back to Hong Kong for another film. It was the last time I saw him alive.

More than twenty thousand grieving fans attended his funeral service in Hong Kong on July 22, 1973. A memorial service was held a few days later in San Francisco. I flew there with Steve McQueen and James Coburn, both of whom had been Bruce's students as well as good friends.

I often think about Bruce and what he might have achieved had he lived. What I recall most vividly, however, were those workouts together in which we both learned from each other. After he left Los Angeles for Hong Kong and the films that would make him famous, Bruce did seem to be always busy, moving around the world with the same speed with which he moved across the mat or the screen. But he always had the time to slow down and share something with a friend, like oranges and Zen riddles.

LET IT GO

Men are like steel. When they lose their temper,

they lose their worth.

The most exciting times of my martial arts career were the team competitions. That was back in the days before safety equipment (the gloves and padding that fighters wear today), and so, bad bruises, even broken bones, weren't all that unusual. Getting hurt was one of the hazards of semi-contact karate competition.

Over a period of years, my team, composed of myself as coach and competitor plus four of my black belts, fought twenty-six teams from all over the country, and we never lost, although we did once come close.

It happened in 1970 during the All-Star Team Championships in Long Beach, California. My team was ahead on points up until the last fight. John Natividad, our least experienced black belt, was scheduled to fight Joe Lewis, who, in addition to being a friend of mine, was also the world champion.

Joe was a formidable opponent for anyone, and each of the members on our team had advice for John, but he said, "Not to worry." However, we were worried, especially when the bout started and Joe came on like gangbusters, hitting John hard and often.

During a break in the match, I knew that John was getting angry and I told him to let it go. "You're letting him get your goat, which is what he's trying to do," I said. "You can't afford to get angry or you'll lose. Anger is self-defeating. I want you to clear your mind of anger and concentrate on why you are here."

I saw the anger in John's eyes dissipate. "You're right," he said. "He's trying to get me to beat myself."

The upshot of the story is that John did let the anger go, and went on to win the match.

I began my competitive career in 1964, winning the professional middleweight championship in 1968 and retired undefeated in 1974 — and devoted myself to my schools. Early one morning in 1972, I got a phone call from Bruce Lee in Hong Kong, offering me a role in *Return of the Dragon,* a film that he was going to make in Rome. My good friend, Bob Wall, was also to have a part in the picture, which was to be his first as well as mine.

Bruce said that he wanted to do a fight scene with me that everyone would remember. I said, jokingly, "Great! Who wins?" He said, "I win. I'm the star." Our fight scene was to be in the Colosseum in Rome. Although Bruce and I had worked out the choreography to a tee, there were constant problems on the set — it took three full days to film just that

one scene — and most of the actors groused about sched-
ules, retakes, and so on. As star of the film, there was more
pressure on Bruce than on anyone else, but somehow or other
he seemed to retain his composure, although I knew that he,
too, was occasionally upset.

One night while having pasta with Bruce at the Tavernia
Flavia in Trastevere, our favorite restaurant, I asked him how
he was able to keep all the stress from upsetting him.

"I have a system of ridding my mind of negative thoughts,"
he said. "I visualize myself writing them down on a piece of
paper. Then I imagine myself crumpling up the paper, lighting
it on fire, and burning it to a crisp. It may seem silly, but the
system works, at least for me."

I have taken Bruce's system one step further. I actually write
down on a scrap of paper whatever negative thoughts I have
and then burn them. When I dispose of the ashes, the thoughts,
too, are removed from my mind. I let them go.

THERE ARE NO
LIMITATIONS

Most people have an image of martial artists as superathletes in the peak of condition, capable of moving effortlessly and quickly, using blindingly fast combinations of skillful techniques to defeat opponents. That image is true for many martial artists, but not for all. Some of the most inspiring men I have ever seen on the mat spin around in wheelchairs before propelling themselves onto their opponent. Others wait patiently and sightless, listening intently for the sound of breathing, thus pinpointing their opponent's position, and then they go into action, substituting their sense of sight for touch.

Frank Ruiz, a leading karate instructor and founder of the *Nisei goju* system in America, is a case in point. "There's only the limitations we place on ourselves," he says, echoing classical Zen thinking.

Frank, a highly decorated Korean and Vietnam War vet, was working as an undercover narcotics agent in New York with JoJo, one of his karate students, as backup. In July 1970, while on assignment, their car had a flat tire on the Cross-

Bronx Expressway. JoJo went out to change the tire but had trouble with the lug nuts. As Frank went out to help, he was hit by a speeding car and thrown a hundred feet into the air.

A doctor stopped, administered CPR, and gave up, pronouncing Frank dead. The ambulance arrived, and Frank was taken to the hospital, where he remained in a coma for five days: Almost every bone in his body was either broken or fractured. The damage his body sustained was equivalent to when falling from a twenty-story building.

When Frank came out of the coma, he was paralyzed from the neck down and told he would never walk again. Doctors said it was a miracle he was alive. The only thing that saved him was his excellent physical condition and the fact that he had instinctively relaxed when thrown up into the air, thanks to his karate training.

Frank made up his mind that he would walk and teach karate again. For hours every day he imagined himself on the mat doing *katas,* practicing techniques, strengthening his body. After five years of therapy and intensive positive imagery, he proved the doctors wrong, finally graduating from a wheelchair to crutches. He even began teaching again.

"We place limitations on ourselves," Frank told me recently. "I lost two legs, so some people call me disabled. But that's just a label. The fact is I can't walk, but I didn't lose my ability to teach. I have no intention of letting a label limit me."

Another man who refuses to be labeled is Ted Vollrath, who, when he was eighteen years old and in the marine corps in Korea, was hit by a mortar shell that shredded his legs so badly they had to be amputated. When he returned home to Harrisburg, Pennsylvania, he decided to learn karate just for exercise. Most instructors seeing him in a wheelchair refused to take him. Ralph Lindquist, a *nishin ryu* instructor, closed his eyes for half a minute, opened them and said, "If you want it, it's there. But you must want it badly." Ted did.

Ted learned to make the wheelchair a weapon, an extension of himself. He uses the armrests as weapons, the footrest for sweeping his opponent's feet off the ground. When he has brought his opponent down, he uses grappling techniques to subdue him.

"If you label yourself as handicapped, you are handicapped, and that's as far as you can go," Ted says. "I'm handicapable."

Today Ted works for Congressman George W. Gekas of the 17th District in Pennsylvania and interviews all prospects for the military academies and congressional appointments. He's also on the Board of Directors for the American Disability Act. His passion, however, is still karate, and he runs Martial Arts for the Handicapable, Inc., a nonprofit organization in Steelton, Pennsylvania.

His students, none of whom pays a fee, include three blind girls — two of them sisters — and two blind young men. He first taught them balance and katas, then *kumite* (free sparring).

"Blind people have a highly developed sense of awareness," Ted says. "I try to help them develop their limitations into strength."

He also gives instruction to black belts from across the nation in techniques for dealing with various types of handicapped students.

Recently Ted was preparing for his one hundred fifty-fifth surgery. "When I come out, I'll pick up where I left off," he told me.

Just knowing such men has been an inspiration to me. They

have succeeded against seemingly insurmountable odds and constant pain.

There have been times in my life when I have been discouraged by problems, and then I think of some of these remarkable men and realize how minor my problems really are. As the Zen masters say, there are no limits for the person who refuses to accept them.

TURNING WORDS

The great swordsman Yagyu Tajima-no-kami became a teacher at the shogun's court. One day one of the shogun's personal guards came to him and asked him to give him training in fencing. The master looked at the man and said, "As I observe, you seem to be a master of fencing yourself. Tell me to what school you belong before we enter into the relationship of teacher and pupil."

The guardsman said, "It shames me to confess it, but I have never learned the art."

"Are you trying to fool me?" asked the master swordsman. "I am teacher to the shogun himself, and I know my eye never fails in its judgments."

"I am sorry to defy your honor," said the guardsman, "but I really know nothing."

The resolute air of the guardsman made the swordmaster think for a while, and he finally said, "If you say so, it must be so. But still I am sure you are a master of something, though I do not know of what."

"If you insist, I will tell you," said the guardsman. "There is one thing of which I can say I am complete master. When I was still a boy, the thought came upon me that as a samurai I ought in no circumstances to be afraid of death, and I have grappled with the problem of death now for some years, and finally the problem of death ceased to worry me. May this be what you sense?"

"Exactly!" exclaimed Tajima-no-kami. "That is what I mean. I am glad that I made no mistake in my judgment. For the ultimate secrets of swordsmanship also lie in being released from the thought of death. I have trained ever so many hundreds of my pupils along this line, but so far none of them really deserves the final certificate for swordsmanship. You need no technical training. You are already a master."

— *related by Daisetz Suzuki*

Enlightenment is the goal of Zen, and meditation is the chosen path. But it is not the only way. Many Zen stories, the famous koans, end with a stock phrase: "And hearing those words he was enlightened." Suddenly hearing certain words, suddenly seeing, as in a flash of light, a larger meaning, can lead to a kind of enlightenment. Such words are often referred to as "turning words" because they are turning points: They turn the listener around and lead him to enlightenment. You might say that turning words give the listener a jolt, suddenly knocking him out of his ordinary patterns of thought into greater consciousness.

I don't claim enlightenment, although I accept it as both the goal of Zen and the primary goal behind much of what people do; we all want to understand ourselves and our lives. Although I don't consider myself enlightened, I have heard words that turned me around, words that jolted me, made me realize I'd been mistaking my view of things for the way things really are or that reminded me of what I already knew but had forgotten.

The essential thing about turning words is that they come from other people. Of course, words from other people can have the power to change our lives without necessarily offering any kind of enlightenment. When someone suddenly announces, "I love you" or "I'm leaving you," you can be sure that your life is in for a change, a real jolt, but you may not experience any sense of greater understanding. With turning words, the difference is that the change occurs only inside you, in how you see yourself and your place in life.

After I officially retired from karate competitions in 1974, I found myself without direction. I had no new goals. As hard as I tried, I could think of nothing new to strive for, and that gave me a sense of listlessness and emptiness. Then, at dinner one night with Steve McQueen, he suddenly asked me why I didn't try acting.

Since I am now an actor, since I'm now as well known as an actor as I am as a martial artist, someone writing a biography of me could point to that moment in that restaurant and claim that Steve's question was an important turning point in my life.

But it really wasn't. You can't live in Los Angeles for years, particularly if you're involved in a line of work that often involves actors — I'd had dozens as students — without thinking about the possibilities of getting into acting. And by the time Steve asked me, I'd already had parts in two films, one with Bruce Lee. The notion of acting had crossed my mind, but that's about all.

The turning words eventually came from Steve, all right, but they came a few months later, when I once again found myself talking with him about my future. I told him I had serious doubts about becoming an actor. After all, Los Angeles is full of unemployed actors (one excellent reason the town is full of good-looking waiters and waitresses), and I'd had no serious acting lessons and had no reason to believe I could ever become an actor.

Then he said, "Remember that philosophy of yours that you always stressed to students: Set goals, visualize the results of those goals, and then be determined to succeed by overcoming any obstacles in the way. You've been preaching this to me for two years, and now you're saying there's something you can't do."

That did it. Those were the words I needed to hear. Steve jolted me back to an awareness of my own beliefs, reminded me of what I myself had been telling other people for years. In so doing, he gave me the goal I had been seeking, and once I had that goal I was on my way. Something else might have come along to push me in the direction of acting — but maybe not, and maybe not as forcefully.

Every worthwhile maxim or technique, whether from Zen or from the martial arts in general, usually deals with one of the two primary relationships in your life: how you relate to yourself and how you relate to others. The two relationships are so close that drawing a line between them eventually becomes impossible. The basic truth is that if you know how to treat, evaluate, criticize, motivate, and reward yourself, you'll be a successfully functional person able to deal effectively and compassionately with the people close to you and with strangers.

And that means, first of all, listening. Steve was a friend, and I took what he said to heart, but those turning words could have come just as easily from a stranger. Or from a child. Almost everyone we meet has something to say, probably even something to teach us. Always be alert to the possibilities in any meeting with a stranger: It can literally change your life.

It also means paying people the respect of taking them seriously. Don't allow yourself to be misled by skepticism about another person's motives. Don't condemn them. Instead, communicate. Turning words are different for each person because we all approach communication with different experiences and different mind-sets, but we must learn to be open to new ideas and thoughts even when they are different or in opposition to ours.

CONQUERING YOURSELF

"Other masters are always carrying on about the necessity of saving everyone," the Zen master Gensha complained to his followers. "But suppose you meet up with someone deaf, dumb, and blind. He couldn't see your gestures, hear your preaching, or, for that matter, ask questions. Unable to save him, you'd prove yourself a worthless Buddhist."

Troubled by these words, one of Gensha's disciples went to consult the master Unmon, who, like Gensha, was a disciple of Seppo.

"Bow, please," said Unmon.

The monk, taken by surprise, obeyed the master's command, then straightened up in expectation of having his query answered.

But instead of an answer he got a staff thrust at him, and he leapt back.

"Well," said Unmon, "you're not blind. Now, approach."

The monk did what was bidden.

"Good," said Unmon. "You're not deaf either. Well, understand?"

"Understand what, sir?"

"Ah, you're not dumb either."

On hearing these words, the monk awoke as from a deep sleep.

~ •

He who conquers himself is the mightiest warrior.

— *Confucius*

Winning is not the basic goal behind martial arts training. The truth — although many people seem to forget it — is that most of the arts are designed to skillfully avoid win-lose situations, to avoid conflict altogether. In the broadest sense, the arts are meant to help people lead happier, more fulfilling lives. Tae kwon do, karate, aikido, judo, arnis, bando, or sumo; they're all much more than methods of self-defense, and as different as their techniques may be, they all lead to a similar goal. In another connection to Zen, that goal is sometimes called "conquering the self."

While it may sound vague, that phrase has real meaning. You "conquer yourself" by recognizing something greater than your personal self. The two basic elements that lead to and reflect that conquest are respect and discipline: respect for yourself, for others, and for your art; discipline in the sense of accepting teaching, abiding by rules, and then applying that to the control of your basic emotions, such as anger and fear.

Many people, particularly young people, find this aspect of

the martial arts hard to grasp. The traits that are valued most highly in a martial artist — courtesy, patience, loyalty, dedication — are not necessarily rewarded in our society today. The people who complain that today's kids have no respect for authority don't always realize that respect, like discipline, is something that is best taught by example, and all too often the right examples are lacking. You can see this in particular in our sports, where the emphasis is on winning, winning at any cost. Even teamwork seems to have fallen out of favor; we put the spotlight on individual stars in their moment of glory.

I know from my own experience, from talking to all kinds of kids all over the country, that kids want — even need — someone or something to respect, a strong idea to hold on to and believe in. In that sense, they're not so very different from most adults. And in that sense, too, study of a martial art can very often fill that need.

Respect begins the first time a martial arts student steps into a dojo and bows to his instructor. Far from being a quaint holdover of Oriental tradition, the bows performed in a dojo are an outward expression of respect for someone in authority, regardless of that person's physical size or age.

The relationship between the instructor, or sensei, and his students is, however, a direct reflection of Oriental tradition. In the East, teachers are looked on with a respect that borders on veneration; students treat their teachers with unquestioning devotion. The relationship between instructor and student resembles the link between a stern father and a son who is totally obedient to his authority. The father-son analogy is apt in several ways, for the martial arts teacher does not stand behind a desk and lecture; rather, he stands in front of his students as the living embodiment of a particular martial art. He teaches not just with words but with his personality, the way he stands and the way he treats his students. In everything he does, he is setting an example for his students to follow. In the simplest terms, the student is in the dojo to become like the teacher, to acquire not just the teacher's technical skills but something of his attitude and character, much as a son grows to resemble his father.

That kind of relationship is hard to establish here in the United States; it seems alien to our way of thinking, but something close to it is required by every martial art. The key to making it work is for the student to take the first step in conquering himself. He must accept that within the walls of the dojo he is a beginner. Unlike studying a creative art such as painting, writing, or playing the piano, which focuses on individual expression, the martial arts student must subjugate his ego in order to learn because the teacher is the art. The teacher stands for everything the student hopes to learn and thus deserves his unstinting attention and respect. If the student can't take this first step and learn respect for the teacher, he'll never learn respect for the art. And by learning respect for the teacher the student acquires a solid goal: to become like his teacher.

Discipline is absolutely demanded by each martial art. Most dojos have basic rules of conduct, either posted on the wall or explained orally, and these rules are strictly enforced. The majority are designed to create the proper atmosphere within the dojo (such as "All uniforms must be clean and in good condition") and within each individual student (such as "Students must always be courteous and helpful"). But there is another kind of discipline in the martial arts, for no student can advance in his training without successfully achieving a series of clearly established levels of proficiency. The tests that must be passed are strict and absolute. There's no such thing as getting by with a barely "passing" grade; either you succeed or you fail and must then practice more before trying again. Each student must have the discipline to follow instructions exactly, to control his personal feelings — to conquer himself yet again — and to accommodate the requirements of his art.

Beginning students often complain that they don't understand why they are being made to perform certain moves, sometimes awkward moves, and why those moves must be executed only in very precise ways; the demands made by the instructor seem unreasonable, based on some outlandish perfectionism. Then the day comes when the instructor has the student put several of those precise, awkward moves together, and the student suddenly finds himself doing something, like a kick that reaches over his head, that he would never have imagined himself capable of doing. On that day all complaining stops, and the student comes to feel an even greater respect for his teacher. I've heard it said that the first period of learning a martial art is like learning to dance, but without a partner and without music, just moving one foot at a time over and over in silence, without knowing why. When you finally add the partner and the music, all those little moves suddenly make wonderful sense.

There is also the discipline demanded by the teacher. Some teachers believe it best to remain aloof, treating their students with a stern politeness that can seem like disdain; others take a more personal approach, and in truth, discipline doesn't have to be harsh. When I started learning a martial art in Korea, there were many days when I really didn't feel like working out. I was tired or bruised, often discouraged because I didn't seem to be improving, and I felt embarrassed when I was on the mat. My instructor recognized my problems and gently encouraged me with small praise such as, "You're beginning to learn," or helpful hints on how I might achieve better focus by relaxing and emptying my mind of everything but what I was doing at the moment. He was instilling discipline, not with the rod and stick, but with gentle affection. Thanks to his teaching and discipline, I went on to get my black belt and to feel better about myself, with a yearning to taste that feeling of accomplishment again.

And that taste of accomplishment, that first sense of personal fulfillment, is much sharper and has more importance because the student is earning praise from an instructor he has come to respect. Because of their shared respect for the art, the student and teacher closely share the student's progress. With each step forward, the student comes closer to the requirements demanded of the art, and in so doing, he also comes closer to his teacher. For the student, the learning becomes a series of realizations or awakenings, all leading to a greater understanding of his art and also of his teacher.

The benefits of respect and discipline are not necessarily glamorous, and they're certainly not immediate, but they are enduring and radiate outward to affect every aspect of the student's life. It should come as no surprise that youngsters who study a martial art usually get better grades in school. In my experience, they're happier overall, better prepared to meet life's challenges, more sure of themselves, and at ease with others.

Of course, the martial arts aren't the only possible ways for a young person to learn respect and discipline. The arts do have certain advantages, however: Most kids are familiar with the moves from television and movies, and the steps up the ladder of learning a martial art are in most cases clearly marked off with colored belts that are a valid source of pride. But there are also organizations that offer very similar benefits, such as the various kinds of scouting, and even serious involvement in a hobby can teach a young person many valuable lessons.

Like most martial artists, I carry the respect and discipline of my art into my daily life. Just as I respect my art, I respect myself and do my best to stay in shape. Unless I'm ill, I work out several hours each day to keep my body toned. I've trained myself to pay close attention to what I eat so I maintain my weight. I believe that similar discipline could help many overweight people: Learning to say no to temptation is really a way of saying yes to what you believe in, to your primary goals. The same applies to alcohol and drugs. I saw more than enough drunks for one lifetime back in Korea, and I've never taken drugs, because they're bad for health, habit-forming, and they impair judgment. Taking care of your body is just an extension of the respect you owe yourself as a practitioner of your art.

I also apply the respect and discipline to my dealings with other people. You might say that the rules of the dojo apply in every room or hallway of life. "Students must always be courteous and helpful," is not a bad idea anywhere and anytime. Martial artists from all over the world tend to exude a kind of affable respect, a calm acceptance of others. I've found the same qualities also in people who have nothing to do with the martial arts but who have found a way of conquering themselves through dedication to some other discipline, some craft or career. In that sense, to conquer yourself means to become like something you admire or respect, for if you seek to live up to your ideals you will eventually become an extension and embodiment of them.

By conquering ourselves, we learn these greater truths — that all people deserve respect and that discipline makes everything possible.

COMPLETE THE WHEEL

It is easy to shield the outer body from poisoned arrows, but it is impossible to shield the mind from the poisoned darts that originate within itself. Greed, anger, foolishness, and the infatuations of egoism — these four poisoned darts originate within the mind and infect it with deadly poison. These three — greed, anger, and foolishness — are, therefore, the sources of all human woe.

— Buddha

I am always impressed at the number of styles most serious martial artists have studied and mastered. Their quest for more knowledge about the arts and themselves seems to be a consuming passion. Pat Strong is a case in point. Pat was one of Bruce Lee's first students in Seattle in 1961. Bruce conducted lessons then in *jun fong* (the original name for the system he later named *jeet kune do*) in the garage of the Blue

Cross building, across the street from Ruby Chow's restaurant, where he worked as a kitchen helper. When Bruce left Seattle for Los Angeles, Pat went on to study and become proficient in hung gar, shoryn ryu, tae kwon do, wing chun, ryukyu kempo, boxing, Gracie Jujitsu, and modern arnis, a Philippine stick-and-knife-fighting art.

When I last saw Pat, he had just returned from Italy as coach of the U.S. team at the World Cup Arnis Championships; the U.S. team won. Like most martial artists, Pat wanted to learn as much as possible about all other styles. Over lunch at a Los Angeles sushi restaurant one day recently, we talked about the various styles we had both studied. We agreed it was important to continue studying, to improve not only our lives but also our abilities.

Pat reached for a napkin and drew a wheel with several spokes. "This represents my martial arts training," he said. "Each spoke in this wheel represents an area of my martial arts training: ground grappling, kicking and punching, joint locking, physical strength, flexibility, conditioning, and mental attitude.

"In order for the wheel to roll smoothly, all the spokes have to be of equal length. Every time I found a weakness, I developed it by studying a new art. My wheel still isn't completely balanced, but it's getting better with each art I study."

As I studied the wheel Pat had drawn, Pat talked about Bruce, who, to most of us in the arts, was the complete martial artist. "Bruce realized he was small, which meant he had to be super fast, so he started to develop his timing by studying boxing and fencing; he knew he wasn't as strong as many of his opponents, so he began to develop his body strength; he wanted to improve his balance, so he studied ballet. Bruce was on a constant journey trying to make his weak spokes strong.

At the same time, he was trying to become fully developed as a person by making each wheel of his life more round."

I remembered that when I had visited Bruce at his home I had been impressed with his personal library, which included books on various subjects, from Zen and Krishnamurti to the laws of physics and popular books on child-raising.

Soon after my conversation with Pat, I had a meeting with one of my former students, who admitted that he was stymied in his ability to improve his technique on the mat. As we talked, I drew a wheel on a piece of paper and labeled each spoke: spinning back kick, wheel kick, lunge punch, back fist, and so on. I asked him to indicate the spokes he thought weak or strong, and suggested that he make the wheel round by working on the weak spokes.

The concept was simple, and he understood it immediately. The next time I saw him on the mat, he was much improved. He had grasped the notion of completing the wheel.

I use the same imagery in my own life. For example, not long ago I realized that I was not accomplishing enough during my workday. I started a daily log of my time and translated the entries as spokes on the wheel. The spokes included time spent on the phone with personal matters and time spent on business; time spent on training; time spent on lunch; time spent in the car traveling to appointments; and time spent actually performing in front of the cameras.

When I drew the wheel, I was amazed to discover that it was totally out of round. As a result, I restructured my day by taking only business calls during the workday and returning personal calls in the evening. I cut my lunch break from an hour to half an hour. I shortened my afternoon nap from half an hour to twenty minutes. Whenever possible, I arranged to have people I needed to talk with come to my office instead of driving somewhere to meet them. With my day better balanced, I started to get more work accomplished and felt better about myself.

I have also applied the wheel technique to my own martial arts training as well as to other areas of my life. For instance, by using the wheel I improved my tennis game: I began to concentrate on my weak backhand to bring it up to par with my stronger forehand. And I have also used it to bring some of my personal and business relationships into better balance.

The concept of the wheel is totally in keeping with the Zen tradition of yin and yang, which suggests that all forces in life are complementary to each other.

CALMING THE
MOVING MIND

A brisk wind was flapping the temple flag, and two monks, watching it, fell into an argument. One said the flag moved, the other held that instead it was the wind that moved. They argued back and forth but could reach no conclusion. Finally, the master appeared and said, "It is not the wind that moves, it is not the flag that moves; it is your mind that moves."

The alarm goes off and you wake up; the phone rings and you answer; you pause too long at an intersection, and the driver behind you honks. All day long bells, whistles, and horns prod us on, keep us moving toward the timely completion of each chore or task. Even in moments of relative silence, our minds rush ahead, checking off the To Do list and planning the rest of the day, breaking it down into hours, sometimes even fifteen-minute segments, usually with some last-minute obligation that needs no reminder since it's been at the back of our mind, nagging, all day long.

It's no wonder that Oriental Zen instructors who come to the United States to teach complain that they have little time for their daily meditation. The average day in the life of the average American leaves little space for any endeavors not directly related to work or the necessary actions of leading a life and running a family.

Telling Americans to slow down seems futile: To slow down means to fall behind, to be late, perhaps to miss some one-time-only opportunity. One of the charming aspects of the past as depicted in books and movies is the amount of time people had to sit and think or talk. People in the past seem to have had more time for the things that matter — for being good and attentive parents, for making lasting friendships and actually enjoying the benefits of loving relationships, for growing personally through study and contemplation.

It's clear from the situations presented in some Zen koans that early practitioners had the time to go off on their own to perfect their methods, to contemplate. Phrases like "after several years" or "many years later" appear in abundance — an archer learned his art, a swordsman became a master, only after periods of time that seem impossibly long to us.

It's difficult to gain perspective on all this precisely because of the difficulties involved in actually slowing down and seeing. Where is the actual movement? What is the real source of the rush? If you look, you'll see that the movement and rush belong to the city, or the office, or the freeway; the stress and the constant push come from the telephones and the clocks and computers. They do not come from you. If you fall in with the sources of movement, letting your mind move at the same speed as the city, if you agree to respond to each impulse, then you, too, will become part of the stress. But nothing obliges you to do so.

You can't slow the city, but you can take control of your life and manage the speed at which it moves. That control begins with yourself, with small matters, the trivial everyday things of your life. If you can control the small things, you'll be better able to control, even to master, the large and important matters that come your way and add stress to your life.

Finding private time is essential for everyone, even children. The Zen masters understood this long ago and from this understanding they developed meditation, which enables the individual to introduce order and calm into the chaos of life. The importance of meditation is unmistakably clear because without meditation, or reflection, often what is learned will be misunderstood or even lost. A calm mind is the real secret to success under stress, because a mind that is not calm will fail to perceive correctly. When you are calm, you can separate and examine your fears and perceptions.

With practice, however, any place can provide a personal sanctuary. I recall a day some years ago when I arrived early for an appointment at the home of a Zen practitioner and heard the raucous sounds of the Bee Gees coming from his study. Although puzzled at his choice of music, I hesitated to interrupt the master and sat down until the music ceased. Finally, at the appointed time, the master came to the door looking at peace with himself and alert as always.

"Why didn't you knock on the door?" he asked me.

"I heard music and thought you were occupied," I replied.

"I was meditating."

"With all that loud music playing?"

The master smiled. "When I am meditating, I don't hear the music," he said.

Noticing the puzzled look on my face, he smiled, and added,

"Sometimes I test my power of concentration. What you heard today was such a test."

"And?" I asked.

"I never heard the music," he said. "When meditating, even the sound of a speeding car is like the sound of a robin chirping."

I meditate when I can find the time, but often in a busy day there are not moments enough to get into a relaxed state for a sustained period of time. So, I have developed my own shortcuts to calming my mind, and that control begins with breathing. I often find it's enough just to take two deep breaths before answering the phone, for in the time of those breaths my body will have had time to relax and my mind will have had time to again return to being in my control — rather than being some tattered banner flapping in the wind.

Private time doesn't have to take place in a room behind a closed door. Time spent thinking, reflecting, and recharging your batteries can take place anywhere where external stimuli cannot intrude on your thoughts.

THE SHADOW WARRIOR

Strategy is the craft of the warrior. This is the way for men who want to learn my strategy:

Do not think dishonestly.

Know the ways of all professions.

Distinguish between gain and loss and worldly matters.

Develop intuitive judgment and understanding for everything.

Perceive those things which cannot be seen.

Pay attention even to trifles.

Do nothing which is of no use.

— *Miyamoto Musashi*

Martial arts lore is replete with stories of the shadow warrior, invariably a menacing character. The most notorious of the shadow warriors was the *ninja,* a practitioner of *ninjutsu,* often translated as "the art of invisibility." Ninjas were credited with being able to vanish in a wisp of smoke, transform themselves into small animals or birds or inanimate objects, be two places at once. They were also skilled masters of disguise, specialists in the art of assassination and fomenting wars, usually leaving no traces behind that would associate them with their foul deeds.

Today the ninja has become a favored heavy in martial arts films. He appears almost as a joke, scurrying around in a head-to-toe black outfit, his face hidden behind a black mask.

But shadow warriors are no joke, especially when they take the form of lawyers, friends, and advisers to one or both of the parties who are having a problem. In that capacity, like the ninjas of legend, the shadow warrior is most often invisible, but the havoc he creates is very real indeed.

One of the problems in dealing with shadow warriors is that their presence may be unknown to you. For example, two acquaintances of mine who had worked long and hard for years to build up their business decided to dissolve their arrangement because one of the partners wanted to retire. They enlisted the services of their accountant, who had been handling their affairs and tax returns for years. As two people who were once good friends, they agreed that it was in their best interests to avoid seeing lawyers if possible because legal fees would diminish their assets.

The accountant was diligent and helpful. He prepared detailed summaries of all the business matters, which he presented to both parties in an impartial manner. But, as time passed, other presumably well-meaning people got into the act, taking sides and giving advice. It seems to be a universal truth that anyone asked for advice on any matter, regardless of how impartial he or she may try to be, is going to try and sweeten the deal for the person asking for advice.

Suddenly there were new issues to discuss, new terms to be met. The shadow warriors, often disguised as friendly kibitzers, had sown the seeds of discord and soon turned friendly ground into hostile territory. Soon, one of my friends began to feel that his partner was stiffing him. In a short time, they were at a stalemate and the matter went to lawyers, then to court. By the time the smoke had cleared, both men, formerly good friends, were enemies.

Another equally common problem was recently faced by a couple I know. They were married for almost two decades when they decided to divorce. There were no children to consider and no third party involved in the decision, just a mutual awareness that the passion had gone from their relationship and a feeling that life had more to offer them than what they were currently experiencing from their marriage. Their assets included a sizable equity in their nicely furnished home and a joint bank account.

After some amicable discussion, they agreed to sell the house, auction off the furnishings, and split the proceeds and their savings right down the middle. "And we didn't need lawyers," the husband told me. "It's great that we can still be friends even though we are getting a divorce."

"No matter if we're divorced, I'll always be there for him," the wife told me in his presence. "And I'll always be there for her," replied the husband.

During lunch a few days later the wife proudly told a friend that she and her husband had achieved the supposedly impossible — an amicable divorce settlement. The friend, a divorcée herself, listened to the brief details and then asked what was going to happen to the household furnishings.

"We're giving everything except our personal belongings to an auction house, and we'll split the proceeds," said the wife.

"Including your Havilland?" the friend asked, referring to a sizable chinaware collection the couple had acquired during vacation trips. "Such a pity," continued the friend. "You'll never get what it's worth."

When she returned home that night, the wife mentioned the chinaware to her husband, and said she would like to keep it. "Okay with me," he said agreeably. "But if you do, I'd like the Seth Thomas grandfather clock."

It was agreed and the matter was dropped until the next day, when the wife reported back to her friend, who promptly said the clock was worth more than the china. "If I were you, I'd have an expert come in and appraise both things so you don't come out on the short end. He may be taking advantage of you."

The wife rose to her husband's defense, saying he would never cheat her. But she did arrange for an appraiser to come to the house. The clock was indeed worth a few hundred dollars more than the china.

After the appraiser left, the wife called her friend and said, "You were right. He was cheating me."

The wife asked a lawyer recommended by her friend to draw up an agreement specifying exactly who was to get what. The lawyer, who was working for an hourly fee, said the agreement would cost only a few hundred dollars. The husband countered by hiring his own lawyer to check out the agreement. There were some problems. Soon the husband was referring to his wife as "that shrew." And so, thanks to the shadow warrior, the battle was joined. The lawyers, one working on a retainer and the other working on contingency, ended up getting the bulk of the couple's estate in fees. And the couple? After a bitter divorce battle, they are no longer speaking to each other, and when they do mention the other, it is always in derogatory terms.

I can't help but think when I reflect on these two situations that no matter how amicable relations are between people — partners, friends, business acquaintances, even spouses — whenever they are considering dissolving a relationship, neither party is without friends and advisers.

How can one avoid the depredations of the shadow warrior? First and foremost, be wary when dealing with someone who has a sudden change of attitude. It is then wise to create good perimeter defenses, and to prepare for an all-out battle because one can never overestimate the damage a shadow warrior can do.

Equally important, don't ever be a shadow warrior yourself. I've noticed that in many languages there is a saying, the gist of which is that you should never place any part of your body between arguing spouses. The fact that such sayings can be found in so many places, and that they're usually of venerable age, only proves their validity. You should always help friends as much as you can, but do so without taking sides and injuring others. Second, never worry about what the people around you are doing or going to do. Worrying will only clog your senses, making you unable to see the situation clearly. The important thing is always what you're going to do; leave any possible shadow warriors out in the dark, where they belong. Third, if a friend seems to be taking someone else's side against you, don't decide that you no longer consider that person your friend. Try to remember the better times of the past, the good feelings you've shared with that person. If you stand firm, loyal to the friendship, the other person will probably come around eventually. Remember that you alone, regardless of how other people — partners, friends, business acquaintances, even spouses — are acting, can keep all conflict to a minimum by acting in a mature manner, by exercising control over both your behavior and your speech. Last, ask yourself what the worst is that could possibly happen. Chances are, the very worst — like having to start over again from scratch — really isn't as bad as you fear. If you look around, you'll see that everywhere are people with problems that make yours seem minuscule.

And if you find yourself encountering real-life black-suited shadow warriors, remember the words of Sun Tzu: "Go to meet those who attack first. Waiting is bad. . . . Observe their attacking order, and go to meet those who attack first."

STANDING TALL

In nineteenth-century Japan, merchants were not highly regarded; in particular it was thought that they lacked courage
and spirit. Some of them naturally resented this and sought to
prove to themselves that it was not so. One merchant even took
lessons at a school of the martial arts in what was then called
torite, mainly methods of disarming and arresting an assailant.
He made remarkable progress, and finally took the degree of
chudan, which represented an expert skill in the art.

One night a thief broke into the merchant's house. Bran-
dishing a knife he demanded money. The merchant refused. The
thief, who was a down-and-out samurai, came at him in a fury
and shouted,

"What, a rat of a merchant standing up to me! I'll rip you
open!"

At the words "rat of a merchant" the merchant broke into a
sweat. His knees trembled, and he was about to ask for mercy.

Then his wife said, "You're not a merchant, you're a chudan of torite."

Suddenly the merchant felt his body straighten up and his legs fill with energy. He jumped at the thief, disarmed him, and threw him out of the house.

Violence is a reality in our lives, whether we experience it directly or only fear it. Terrible things seem to happen every day, not just in foreign countries but here in the United States, sometimes just around the corner.

Most Americans wish there was something they could do to bring an end to such problems; I know I do. A few years ago someone jokingly told me that everything would be better if I would just agree to teach every single American karate. He was only joking, of course, but he wasn't all that wrong. Everything wouldn't be better if I taught everyone the kicks and punches of karate — few problems can be resolved that way — but things would improve to an enormous degree if everyone learned something of the discipline and respect that is the base of martial arts.

Inevitably, perhaps, I'm often asked what I'd do if a gang of muggers demanded my wallet. The question is based on faultless logic: The martial arts are methods of self-defense, and knowledge of martial arts is considered an essential element in the training of soldiers, law enforcement officials, and bodyguards worldwide. A highly trained martial artist like me is in a very real sense a lethal weapon. Even so, I always give the same answer to the question: If confronted by a gang of muggers, I'd hand over my wallet.

It would be different, of course, if it was a matter of saving a life — including my own. In that case, I'd go all out. But the contents of a wallet aren't worth risking a life, aren't worth getting hurt or injuring someone else.

In reality, serious martial artists don't spend years studying and practicing just to turn themselves into lethal weapons. I originally got into karate because it offered me things that nothing else did — a sense of accomplishment, a sense of self-worth. The more I learned, the more assertive and communicative I became, the better I felt about myself, physically and emotionally. What really changed my life was earning my black belt. It was the first time that I had accomplished something difficult on my own, and that one success made me eager for more. I wish everyone could experience that sense of self-esteem and satisfaction by setting meaningful goals and achieving them, because one goal makes the next one possible and brings home the concept of success. For once you've truly succeeded in accomplishing one goal, you're eager to move ahead to others.

Martial arts, both as physical training and as philosophical outlook, helped me achieve success, and from that success I went on to my career in films. I try to say something in my films, of course, something that I hope is understood by those who see them, namely, that violence is only the last resort, that a true hero tries other means first. In that sense, I intend the heroes of my films to be seen as symbols of the United States, stand-ins for all of us.

I'm often given the opportunity to speak to underprivileged youngsters, an opportunity I value because it gives me the chance to speak to them directly, to tell them what I believe. Whether they recognize me as Chuck Norris the martial artist, the actor, or see me as just an action hero — James J. McQuade, Colonel James Braddock, or Walker, Texas

Ranger — they listen to me. So I tell them the truth, which is, that they can all be successful, that they can all achieve their goals if they are positive in everything they do.

When I have an opportunity for face-to-face meetings with youngsters, I stress the importance of better posture, by which I mean not just standing straight but also having a solid mental posture — standing tall inside themselves. I try to teach them how to avoid conflict, the primary goal behind all martial arts. And I try to teach them control, the inner control that comes with being physically and psychologically centered.

Who knows? If I could get the ear of enough students, then violence would have no place except on the mat, where it serves to teach us lessons to better our skills. In my films and television show, I try to entertain with a moral: that right-minded people stand up for themselves and never abuse the rights of others.

THE TOP OF THE FIST

One night when master Taigan was reading a book, a thief came into his room carrying a big sword. Looking at the thief, the master asked, "Which do you want: money or my life?" "I came for money," replied the thief. Taigan took out his purse and handed it to the man, saying, "Here it is." Taigan then returned to reading his book as if nothing had happened to him. The thief began to feel ill at ease and left the room overawed. "Hey! Wait a minute," called Taigan. The thief stopped, something in Taigan's voice causing him to shudder. "Why don't you shut the door?" asked Taigan. Days later the thief was captured by the police and said, "I've been robbing for years, but I've never been so terrified as when that Buddhist priest called after me, 'Hey, wait a minute.' "

The so-called past is the top of the heart; the present
is the top of the fist; and the future is the back of the
brain.

— Zen saying

Life comes to us one day at a time. Thanks to the movement of the earth, every twenty-four hours we are presented with a new morning, a new beginning to life, a completely new day in which to become ourselves and discover what life has to offer.

That's the simple truth — each day is a new beginning — but making use of it, living up to what it offers, can be anything but easy. Each morning, just as soon as you open your eyes, an enormous weight falls onto you once again, sometimes in the form of remembering what the day has in store — maybe some problem at work, a deadline to meet, too many places to be at the same time — and sometimes in the very solid form of an enthusiastic and rambunctious child. I'll never forget the morning I woke up with a bad headache and my nose broken from a karate match. My son Eric, who was three at the time, began bouncing up and down on the bed and, of course, landed square on my nose, breaking it once again.

Every morning all the problems and responsibilities, all the memories come rushing back. After my brother Wieland was killed in Vietnam, for a long time he was my first thought each and every morning, and those thoughts stopped me in my tracks. I still think of him every day, he's inside me when I wake up.

And when I wake up these days, as often as not I'm in Texas, working on *Walker, Texas Ranger*. That's because I'm an actor; I had the broken nose that morning long ago because I'm also a martial artist; Eric is in this world because I'm a husband and father; and Wieland and Aaron are with me because I'm a brother. I'm also a writer and director and an off-road racer. And so on.

We have a saying about wearing many different hats, and the truth is, we all have a closet full of them. All of us must "perform" different characters during the day — father, brother, businessman, friend — according to what we're doing, who we're with. Calling those different roles "hats" can actually be helpful, because it makes you realize that one person is donning and doffing all the hats, and that one person is something more than the roles being played. That one person is all the roles mixed together with memories of the past and hopes and dreams for the future. Of course, sometimes the roles we're forced to play are unpleasant, or at least not ones we would have chosen ourselves, and at such times it's best to remember good times and to trust as well that better times are to come if you make them.

I'll never forget the year 1970, the year Wieland died and also the year my career headed suddenly upward. I was thirty years old that year, I had a new house and a new car — a gold Cadillac Coupe deVille — I had a big office in the Union Bank Building in Torrance, California, and a job as an executive for a big corporation. I had all that because the corporation in Torrance had bought up the karate schools I ran in partnership with my friend Bob Wall. In terms of progress up the ladder of life, I was climbing high, and I woke up each morning looking forward to another day's activity.

The fall came only three years later, when the big corporation found itself in financial difficulties and sold the schools to another company, which then turned around and sold them to someone who ran them right into the ground. So I bought back the schools, and when I did so I suddenly found myself way over my head in debt. I consulted a businessman, explained my situation, and he went over all the numbers, checked into all the angles and possibilities, and then told me it was impossible. He said I had to declare bankruptcy, that there was no other way.

That was something I simply couldn't do. It went against something deep inside me, something more important even than my personal pride. I fought back. The Cadillac was soon gone, and I nearly lost the house, too. The time came when I was completely broke. Those were trying times, among the hardest I've ever known, and when I woke up every morning I wasn't happy with what I had to remember about the coming day.

But I never permitted myself negative thoughts, and when the going really got rough I found that my friends stood by me, doing whatever was within their means. In the end I was successful. And when I'd climbed my way back up, I realized that I'd been successful in several senses. I had paid back the creditors every cent and had my schools again, which was certainly one big success; but I'd also been helped by my friends — I'd seen sure proof of the true meaning of friendship — and I'd come to know myself better, for struggling against adversity throws a sharp light on character. Perhaps the biggest success of all was that I'd also seen proof that if you want something deep in your heart you can accomplish it, even if it seems impossible, even if the people around you tell you to your face that it's impossible.

Was I aware of Zen during those hard days? Maybe not, but what I was doing by keeping my eyes focused straight ahead and not permitting myself to dwell on negative thoughts was certainly in keeping with the teaching of Zen. Although many people don't realize it, Zen is not about monks meditating as much as it is about taking action, making decisive moves in the present. There's a certain impatience about Zen, an unwillingness to get lost in meandering arguments, a desire to cut quickly to the essential, or to "get to the bottom line." And if the bottom line is against you, remember that today is only one day, no matter how hard, and tomorrow is always more than a promise: It's a guarantee.

YOUR MASTER,
YOUR ART

Behind every great master of every art, sport, or subject is a teacher, and that teacher, in turn, was a beginning student before becoming a teacher. Awareness of the credentials and lineage behind almost every teacher should be of great comfort to all of us, for it reflects the fact that at one time or another everyone was nothing more than a beginner and that learning continues throughout a lifetime, from the preschool years on.

Because of this handing on from teacher to student to teacher, behind every art is a row of masters, a succession of teachers and students, that leads back, in many cases, to the very beginning of the art in question.

The time came, back when I was competing in martial arts tournaments, when I could no longer surprise opponents with the techniques I had learned in Korea, so I decided to increase my repertoire. To do so, I studied with other leading karate instructors. One of the people I went to was Hidetaka Nishiyama, a famous karate instructor. Nishiyama began his karate training in Japan under Gichin Funakoshi — the man regarded as the founder of modern karate — and Funakoshi had in turn studied with Yasutsune Azato and Tasutsune Itosu. In a sense, the hand and foot combinations I learned from Nishiyama had been handed down from the beginnings of karate. I also studied with Ed Parker, one of the leading karate instructors in this country and the father of American *kenpo* karate. Parker was born in Hawaii, where he studied with William Chow; Chow leads back to his master, James Mitose, who in Japan had studied the Shao-lin kung fu originally taught by the fifth-century Buddhist priest known as Bodhidharma, who brought to China the combination of yoga and Indian fistfighting that became the Shao-lin system. My good friend Bruce Lee began his studies in Hong Kong with Yip Man, Grand Master of the wing chun style of kung fu. Master Man began his kung fu training with Chan Wah Shun at age thirteen. At sixteen he moved to Hong Kong, where he studied wing chun under Leung Bik.

There's a saying that "even the masters have masters." It may seem obvious, but the meaning runs deeper in the martial arts due to the particular way in which they are taught; teaching a martial art is far different from teaching an academic subject like political science or economics. In the broadest sense, the martial arts teacher doesn't so much teach as "hand on," and what he hands on to the student is not information, not intellectual data, but something deeper, something best described as spiritual. The kind of intellectual data a schoolteacher teaches can easily be detached from the personality of the teacher himself, so that in time the student may well forget the teacher and remember only the information. In truth, any other teacher could have taught the same material. In the case of the martial arts teacher, what is taught — or handed on — is tied inseparably to the teacher. In a very real sense, your master is your art.

There are other ways in which the relationship between the teacher and student is different in the martial arts. In an academic setting, the teacher refers to books or other sources, in a sense doing his best to rework the information to make it understandable to the student. The martial arts teacher refers only to his own experience, for he is helping his student follow a path that he, the teacher, has himself followed, step by step. This makes for a close relationship between the student and the teacher.

Martial arts students are often astonished at how much their teachers seem to understand about them; it seems almost that the teacher already knows what the student will do, where the student will have difficulty, even what the student is thinking. And, of course, the teacher does know, for he has done and thought those same things in the same way. This closeness helps inspire the respect that students have for their teachers, and this respect is not just for the teacher, but for the discipline itself, for what is being handed on.

When competitors meet at tournaments, they frequently identify themselves by identifying the dojo where they studied and the name of their instructor. The basic truth is that the practitioners of martial arts are performing skills they were taught. Although each martial artist may seek to perfect some technique and put his own stamp on it — like my spinning back kick — the art itself had to be learned from someone else.

People often remark on the fact that most leading martial artists are not just performers, not just competitors, but also teachers and quite often also the authors of books on their discipline. The urge to teach, to pass on the art, is very much an inherent part of the martial arts. In a very real sense, each student becomes a teacher as soon as he or she reaches a certain level because they have knowledge that can be passed on.

The fact is, however, that the student who is awarded a first-degree black belt is akin to a new college graduate: He or she is at the beginning again, ready now for advanced study. In essence, in all avenues of life we are always at the beginning, preparing to go forward, for when we start at the beginning our knowledge grows. The concept is pure Zen and shows up in the martial arts in the system of colored belts used to indicate the rank achieved, from the white belt of the beginner to the black belt of the teacher. This progression reflects the fact that early students of martial arts were prohibited from washing their belts; therefore they grew steadily darker over the years of sweat and soiling. But a black belt doesn't stay black. With more years of use, it begins to wear away and fray, returning to its original whiteness as the master himself, through constant learning, finds himself ready to begin once again.

CLIMBING THE
INNER MOUNTAIN

Zen in its essence is the art of seeing into the nature of one's own being, and it points the way from bondage to freedom. By making us drink from the fountain of life, it liberates us from all the yokes under which we finite beings are usually suffering in this world.

— Daisetz T. Suzuki

Everything that has been achieved is merely a preliminary exercise for the achievements to come, and no one — not even one who has reached perfection — can say he has reached the end.

— Eugen Herrigel

When is the moment of victory? When do you finally know you are a success? Too many people think that moment comes only when the final bell rings or whistle blows, only when the winning player shakes hands with the defeated, only at the very end of the contest.

The truth is something else altogether. The truth is that you become a winner long before the big contest begins, certainly not during it and not when it's over. You become a winner by playing with honest effort, by putting into the contest everything you have. If you don't get into the game, you can neither play nor win.

Zen teaches us that working toward a goal is often more rewarding than actually achieving it. Possession of the goal is what changes everything, illuminating your path and giving you inner direction: Without a goal to strive for, your talents may well remain undiscovered, even to yourself. Without a goal, your potential, however great, will be just that and nothing more, a potential, something that always might have been.

I've never met Reinhold Messner, the world's greatest living mountaineer, but I'd like to because of what he said about what he was thinking while climbing some of the world's highest peaks. "In my climbing," Messner said, "I am going practically with my feet and body in a place like the top of Everest — but this is only the outside world. In the same moment, I climb my inner mountain.

"More and more I understand how limited I am. As human beings we have problems. We have fear. . . . I am not seeking to achieve a summit, I am searching to achieve more knowledge about my fears and hopes and about being a human being."

What Messner says about "climbing the inner mountain" is totally in the Zen tradition; his concept certainly applies to the real goal of competition even when competing with others; to truly win you must compete with yourself, for the true successes in life are achieved on that "inner mountain." It is the steps we take up that slope that really matter. We're all a little like Messner: We move ahead through life, we move upward along a certain route, but while we do so, we're aware at times of another movement, an inner movement.

As Messner slowly makes his way up the mountain toward his outer goal — the peak, the summit — he must constantly confront his inner fears, his awareness of the very real danger he is in, his sense of his own physical limitations. With each movement up the mountain, he must overcome not just the physical reality, another stretch of ground, but his own inner blocks, including, perhaps, the belief that what he is trying to accomplish may well be impossible. When the goal is achieved and he reaches the top, he has succeeded in two ways, and who is to say that the inner victory wasn't the greater?

Messner learns as he climbs. As he makes his way up the mountain, his view beneath him changes; he can see more of what is around him and his sense of where he is and what really exists in the world around him increases.

The depth of vision we get from experience, the increased sense of self we get from facing up to fears, the values we learn the "hard way" are the steps we take up the inner mountain as we're climbing up the outer mountain of life. Our progress up that inner mountain is harder to gauge because there are no easily recognizable signposts along the way to measure our movement. What is the ultimate goal? Where is success?

Schoolchildren are fortunate, though they certainly wouldn't see it that way, always complaining about how much homework they have. They're fortunate in the sense that their goals are laid out for them, the route upward is clearly marked off. They are literally led along from level to level toward a series of goals: to finish grade school, to finish junior high, to graduate from high school and get that diploma. At each step along the way they know where they are and where they're going, and their progress at school is usually accompanied by physical growth. They can actually see themselves changing, getting bigger as they move ahead.

Many people choose to continue up that ladder by going on to college, where every level, from freshman to senior, has a name, and there is again a clearly defined goal at the end, a piece of paper with their name on it. All those goals offer moments of victory to celebrate, days to smile for the camera, and those snapshots in the scrapbook — high school graduation, college graduation — become like the pencil lines scratched on the inside of a doorjamb, measurements of growth.

Once they get off that educational ladder, many people climb onto the corporate ladder, where their upward progress is marked by changes in title, raises in salary, maybe a new office on the corner with a window and a view. And as they move along that route, they pass other signposts: They get married, become parents, buy a new house, buy a new car — maybe even right off the showroom floor — then suddenly find themselves alone in the house again, and maybe even grandparents.

And that is success. To get up and go to work every day and do a job well and to raise and care for a family should be recognized as the true success it is. Too many people undervalue that, too many fail to realize the true worth of those accomplishments.

Some people never achieve much success on life's outer mountain. In the eyes of others, they fail to amount to much. But I've often found that such people have achieved that other success, they've climbed high up the inner mountain, and such people have much to offer: a broader vision, a deeper understanding.

That kind of vision and that depth of understanding are available to all of us, for all around us every day people are performing large and small miracles of the spirit. And those miracles bring me right back to mountains and to a man named Norman Vaughan. Back in 1928, Mr. Vaughan left college so he could participate in Admiral Byrd's exploration of Antarctica. In recognition of Vaughan's contributions to the expedition, Byrd named a 10,302-foot mountain for him. And sixty-two years later, Vaughan became the first man to reach the top of that very mountain. He accomplished this seemingly impossible goal just three days before his eighty-ninth birthday and despite the fact that he had never climbed a mountain before, that the wind gusted up to sixty miles per hour, that he has an artificial right knee and a right-angle joint that does not bend, and despite the fact that midway up the mountain he was forced to stop temporarily by snow blindness.

Vaughan's triumph and those of Messner are an inspiration to me because they give credence to my personal philosophy, based on learning from Zen, that if you want something deep in your heart you can accomplish it, even if it seems impossible, even if the people around you tell you to your face that it's impossible. Just by having the goal, you're already a winner and well on your way up the inner mountain.

A Zen monk has no car because he has chosen to travel another route. Most of us have cars, new ones, when we're doing well, but we shouldn't use them to measure our forward progress, and we should learn to recognize and celebrate our inner, personal triumphs.

Ki:
THE UNIVERSAL POWER

The Zen masters believe that the way of the universe is a way of remaining in balance and in harmony with nature. Moving with and not against energy can open the creative paths of the mind. You will then be at one with the universe. In the truest Zen sense, you will be the center of the universe, no matter where you are or the circumstances you find yourself in.

This source of inner power, called *ki,* is an invisible life force that flows throughout the universe and that, given the proper training and practice, is available to everyone on demand. Ki flows through each of us, passing through an area of the body called the *tai-ten,* or "one point," which is the gravitational center of the human body and is usually about an inch and a half below the navel. By being "centered" — being focused and in touch with that "one point" — we can make use of this universal energy.

We all have that source of power within us, although most of us have never used it, but it is available on demand. For example, a child is pinned beneath a car, and its mother, a frail woman, is somehow able to harness the strength to lift the car up to set her child free. Under ordinary circumstances she could never do this, but in this instance, without even being aware of it, she used ki.

The fact is that everyone has ki, which is really little more than a technique of visualization allowing one to utilize the internal energy that we all have and letting it flow through the body, as the mother did when lifting the car.

Martial artists learn how to harness their ki under ordinary circumstances. Koichi Tohei, a disciple of Morihei Ueshiba, founder of aikido, tells of going to the mountains, where the temperature is in the low teens, with a group of adherents. Even though the water in the mountain rivers is nearly freezing, the group is able to stay immersed for several minutes at a time by mentally preparing themselves and projecting ki. This is not a matter of ignoring the cold but of having the body and mind totally integrated.

In my tape library is an old film of Ueshiba, taken when he was in his late seventies. In it, he is attacked by several much larger and burlier men, and he throws them around as though they are children with simple movements of his hand using his ki. Sounds impossible? It's not. It's practiced use of ki.

To demonstrate the concept of ki to new students, I hold an arm straight out from my body at a ninety-degree angle and ask the student to walk directly into my arm and try to go past it. In all probability, the arm will stop their progress. I then ask the student to try again, but this time to project his or her thoughts beyond my extended arm. Invariably they can walk right through it without effort.

Almost everyone has seen karate demonstrations in which martial artists break boards, cinder blocks, or bricks with chops or kicks. I've done it lots of times, and although I've sometimes had the uneasy sense that I was performing in a kind of circus act, I knew it served a valid purpose by giving people a dramatic and memorable demonstration of the power of ki.

The technique is simple because, by directing my ki to the far side of a brick or cinder block I am thinking through the block and visualizing my hand going through it. (A warning here: Please don't try this on your own until you have mastered ki.)

By using his ki, Bruce Lee, who weighed around 150 pounds, was able to knock a 250-pound man backward several feet with a punch that traveled less than two inches. Bruce was a paradox, a small man who could easily defeat a giant with skill, speed, and extraordinary power. The power came from his highly developed use of ki.

Ki is natural to everyone, even an infant, as every parent knows. A child who does not want to be lifted is far heavier when he is not cooperating but far lighter when he wants to be picked up. The reason: When not cooperating, the child instinctively projects his ki downward, coordinating the mind and body.

It's clear that learning a martial art involves coming into possession of a certain amount of powerful force. Looked at that way, you'd expect martial arts masters — the men who have dedicated their lives to perfecting that force — to be fire-breathing behemoths bending iron bars over their heads. Instead, they're often the calmest and quietest men in a room. Nor are they always large and muscular: Bruce Lee was certainly no stand-in for Hercules, but he was one of the strongest men I've ever met, and extremely knowledgeable about Zen. He was a true scholar.

The sense of calm that surrounds most martial artists is a result of their being centered. And the movements of an experienced practitioner, whether performing an exercise or engaging in a bout, have a deliberate sense — even when performed with lightning speed, they are coordinated and balanced — precisely because they are in accordance with the flow of energy coming from within but also passing through.

There's more to ki, however, than just projecting power. In my daily life I use ki to center myself mentally and physically, thus calming and preparing myself to deal with any eventuality. I "think through" the problem to find the solution.

MY WAY OF
MEDITATING

All that we are arises

With our thoughts —

With our thoughts

We make the world.

— Buddha

One of the obligatory scenes in many martial arts movies comes before an important action sequence, when the hero sits passively and quietly in a position of meditation. He is calming his mind and body before he must physically exert himself to the utmost. For example, in *Enter the Dragon,* when Bruce Lee is discovered in a shaft by the heavies, he sits cross-legged with his *nunchakus* draped over his shoulders, totally relaxed and at peace with himself and his surroundings even though he is in immediate danger.

I recall that Bruce insisted on that moment in the film because he wanted to get some hint of Zen into what was otherwise an action movie. Bruce knew that Zen translates as "meditation" in Japanese and he was intent on adding dimension to his character.

Unfortunately, there is a great deal of nonsense clouding meditation, which is not some Oriental gimmick but a very sensible method of first concentrating and then clearing the mind to bring it into focus. Meditation is also like a restful sleep that calms the buzzing in your brain.

Meditation is a primary part of the Zen student's activity. In traditional Zen meditation, students in monasteries often concentrate on seemingly impossible questions called *koans,* actually bits of nonrational questions, such as, "How can you go farther from the top of a hundred-foot pole?" or "What is the sound of one hand clapping?" There is no trick answer to such questions; in fact, there is no one single "correct" answer at all. The point is to meditate on the question. But the truth of a koan — like the truth of Zen itself — cannot be reached by logical reasoning.

Long meditation on a koan can almost be mentally painful: Hour after hour, the student approaches the question again and again, from every angle, prodding with his mind in search of a possible answer. The koan itself can begin to feel like an enormous stone block against which all reasoning crumbles. You could also say that the koan is a stumbling block purposely put in the way of the student by his master. The master, after all, is teaching what cannot be taught; he uses the koans to lead the student astray, to push him aside, so that the student will be forced to find his way to the truth alone.

That concept is too esoteric for me personally and most of the Zen practitioners I know, although I have no doubt that the best martial artists understand something of Zen and practice meditation. I insist that my own students spend a few minutes before and after each session meditating to clear their minds. The Zen masters believe that meditation is a practice that builds the patient, calm, and undisturbed peace of mind essential to recharging one's batteries.

There are very precise rules for meditation, but since not everyone has the time or even the ability to perform them, they can be modified, even to the point where they are no longer related to the basic rules. Nonetheless, they remain a valid method for achieving the same results. It is the content of Zen meditation that matters, not the style or the trappings.

The key to meditation begins with breath control. I first became acquainted with controlling my breathing when I was studying martial arts in Korea. Often it was bone-chillingly cold and rainy with icy winds, and we were dressed lightly, even though we were out of doors. All lessons began with breathing exercises, and I soon discovered that as the breathing exercise progressed, I became warm and my body relaxed.

As for myself, I make it a practice to meditate for ten minutes every morning and in the evening, when the day is done. Before going into difficult business meetings I always meditate for a few minutes whenever possible.

My own system is to find a place where I can be comfortable and free of interruption. It is important to be comfortable because a primary part of meditation is breathing, which is meant to induce complete relaxation of the body.

Whenever possible, I like to meditate in the early morning, before sunrise if possible. I go to my workout room and, although it has windows facing broad expanses of pasture, some trees, and horses grazing in the distance, I face a blank wall, so I won't be distracted. There is no phone in the room, so I won't be interrupted. I then sit cross-legged on the floor (some people prefer to sit with legs half-crossed or on a chair) with my hands loosely in my lap, the thumbs touching. My eyes are directed at the floor, to a point three feet in front of me.

I begin by concentrating on my breathing, which starts from deep within the abdomen — much like the breathing a baby engages in. Only when we get older do we learn to breathe from the chest. It is important to concentrate on the act of breathing itself because concentration is the crux of meditation. As the mind is allowed to focus on a single thing, it stills. As the mind is kept in the present, it becomes calm. The key to meditation is concentration.

I breathe in and out in a natural rhythm, with each breath drawn consciously and counted. Breathing out is done with emphasis. The more you concentrate on your breath — not think about your breath, but concentrate on it — the more oblivious you will be to external distractions, and soon you will not be aware of them and will begin to relax. When lapses in concentration occur, when a disturbing or irrelevant thought intrudes on my consciousness, I just start counting my breaths again.

In time you will ignore your breathing as it finds its own rhythm, at which point the outside world will be shut out and the inside world will begin to wake up. It is only then that I try to concentrate on a pleasant image or a phrase or problem. The answer to a problem begins with seeing that it is really in my mind, and not something external.

As you learn to keep your mind in the present, ignoring the past and the future, you should discover the inner resources to deal with whatever has been troubling you. When the mind is calm, it is easier to distinguish between real and imagined problems. You will find a way either to change the circumstances or to change your thinking about the source of your problem.

Years ago when I was competing in martial arts tournaments, I used that breathing technique to calm myself before going on the mat; other thoughts were kept from my mind, and with total concentration on breathing, I soon relaxed and was able to compose my mind.

As an actor-producer-writer of my own films and television series, I am often confronted with situations involving many people, some of them angry, belligerent, or defensive, and everyone looking to me for a solution to the problem. When that happens, I control my breathing, and it always restores calm, confidence, and strength. It also allows me to bring my emotions and thoughts under control, so that I can concentrate on what's at hand.

Many people believe that the purpose of meditation is to solve a problem. They attempt to achieve a meditative mood and then concentrate on what is disturbing them, hoping they will resolve the issue. In my view, that defeats the purpose of meditation.

When I am meditating I am able to seal myself off so completely from reality that I become impervious to all sorts of external problems, such as physical discomfort, pain, and mental anguish. For me the act of meditation is the act of clearing and calming my mind. I am not in a monastery. I am a contemporary man living a full life, and Zen is part of my life, not a replacement for it.

YESTERDAY I HAD
TOMORROW

Ikkyu, the Zen master, was very clever even as a boy. His teacher had a precious teacup, a rare antique. Ikkyu happened to break this cup and was greatly troubled. Hearing the footsteps of his teacher, he held the pieces of the cup behind him. When the master appeared, Ikkyu asked: "Why do people have to die?"

"This is natural," explained the teacher. "Everything has to die and has just so long to live."

Ikkyu, producing the shattered cup, added: "It was time for your cup to die."

The masters say, "Zen is," and that's all, there's no further elaboration. I've always been intrigued by the simplicity of Zen — so often just a few words, no more than the absolute minimum number needed, are able to express a great deal more than you'd expect. That simplicity is one of the defining characteristics of Zen, but it also shows up far away from Zen masters: You can also find it in children. Children seem able to grasp the philosophical core of Zen even though in almost all cases they've never even heard the word. It comes down to simple honesty, really. Children speak directly from their experience, without any of the "blocking" the rest of us have to learn to avoid. They are also able to accept the inevitabilities, even the cruelties, of life without the consternation and even rage so often expressed by adults in similar situations. Sometimes, in fact, it seems that no Zen master can put life in better perspective than a young person. I know because I've met some wonderful kids over the years.

I'm an avid supporter of the Make-A-Wish Foundation, an organization dedicated to helping terminally ill children achieve a wish. Last year I got a call from the foundation telling me that a nine-year-old boy in Philadelphia who was dying of cystic fibrosis had asked to meet me.

I called and arranged to visit the boy at home. I took with me some pictures and a jacket emblazoned with "Walker, Texas Ranger," the kind of jacket members of the TV crew wear.

When I arrived, I found the boy in bed, tubes attached to him at various places helping him breathe and providing nourishment to his frail body. His mother removed a ventilator tube so he could speak. I didn't want to tire him out, so I answered his questions in depth but kept my own questions brief.

His mother whispered to me that the doctors had told her it would be only a few months before he died, and he knew it, but she felt that he had made his peace with God and was unafraid to die.

"How long can he last?" I asked.

The boy, who must have overheard our whispered conversation, rasped, "Yesterday I had tomorrow."

It was only as I was driving back to my hotel that I thought over what the dying boy had said and realized that in those few words he had expressed a simple concept worthy of any Zen master.

There's more to Zen than philosophy, of course, and there's more to the martial arts than Zen. In the end Zen is a way of life and also a way of looking at life. Martial artists love sharing their wealth — the wealth that comes from being involved in a discipline that is both physically and mentally rewarding — and something special happens when you put children together with martial artists.

Last year I received a telephone call from a young mother who told me that her son was dying of a brain tumor. A fan of the Ninja Turtles, he wanted more than anything else to learn martial arts, even though he was growing steadily weaker. I had just planned an instruction seminar for my black belts to be followed by a tournament, so I invited him to be my guest. I felt he would be interested not only in the activity but also in the question-and-answer period, in which I try to bring some Zen philosophy into my responses. The gist of my answers always is to avoid confrontation whenever possible, although I sometimes demonstrate ways that I would physically handle a particular situation, such as dealing with two or more opponents armed with weapons.

I informed all my instructors about the boy, and they gave him a gi to wear along with an honorary black belt. One of the instructors showed him some basic moves, and he did them as best he could with unbridled happiness shining in his face. That evening he sat in a front row seat during the tournament, cheering and laughing. Later on, we had an awards dinner, and the tournament winner gave the youngster his trophy.

The boy was thrilled. "This has been one of the happiest times of my life," he told me as I drove him to the airport the next day. The last time I saw him he was boarding the plane clutching the trophy. A few months later his mother called to say that her son had died.

"Even in his hospital bed, he kept practicing some of the moves he had been shown because he didn't want to forget them," she said. "Up until the very end he said that he was going to study the martial arts when he got better. That visit with you, and the inspiration he got from his lessons, kept him alive a few months longer."

A few years ago I helped organize the Kick Drugs out of America Foundation, an organization designed to work with high-risk inner-city children. The idea is to teach the kids martial arts to help raise their self-esteem and instill discipline and respect for themselves and others. Many of the kids, boys as well as girls, come from broken homes and are having trouble both in school and in their lives in general. I'm pleased to say that the program has been working phenomenally well — most young people quickly adapt to the philosophy of the arts.

Sometimes students are sent to us for disciplinary problems. A teenage boy in Galveston, Texas, had beaten up his school teacher and then proceeded to kick in the teacher's car. The boy was a gang member, he'd been in trouble before, and he was due to be sent to reform school since he was considered incorrigible. One of his instructors intervened, however, and convinced the authorities to put the boy on probation and in our program.

A year later I received a letter from the boy's mother. She

wrote that while her son was in the gang, he and his friends would come to her house, tear it up, and terrify her. He'd had to quit the gang as a condition of joining our program. In only a few months he went from failing grades to a C average, and when he went home, he sometimes took his karate team with him, and they were all respectful. "Your program has turned him around. Thank you for saving his life."

After more than thirty-five years in the martial arts, competing and training thousands of young people, there is one story that is engraved in my memory. It was told to me by Alice McCleary, one of my instructors.

One of her young students showed up for training class without his purple belt. Alice reminded him that part of his responsibility as a student was to have his gi and belt with him at all times.

"Where is your belt?" she asked.

The boy looked at the floor and said he didn't have it.

"Where is it?" Alice repeated.

"My baby sister died, and I put it in her coffin to take to heaven with her," the boy said.

Alice had tears in her eyes as she told me the story. "That belt was probably his most important possession," she said.

The boy had learned to give his best, a lesson he had probably learned from Alice, from martial arts and from Zen which teaches us when to accept things and how to make peace with the inevitable, such as serious illness or death.

HOW TO LIVE
BETTER AND LONGER

Zen master Tenno Dogo (T'ien Tao-wu) had a disciple called Soshin. When Soshin was taken in as a novice, he expected lessons in Zen from his teacher, much as a schoolboy would be taught in school. But Dogo gave him no special lessons, which left Soshin confused and disappointed. Finally, he said to the master, "It is some time since I came here, but not a word has been given me regarding the essence of the Zen teaching."

Dogo replied, "I have been giving you lessons in Zen discipline ever since you first arrived here."

"What kind of lessons were those?"

"When you bring me a cup of tea in the morning, I take it; when you serve me a meal, I accept it; when you bow to me I return it with a nod. How else do you expect to be taught in the mental discipline of Zen?"

⌣•

I have realized that the past and
the future are real illusions,
that they exist only in the present,
which is what there is
and all there is.

— *Alan Watts*

When I was in high school I thought that some of my teachers, who were probably only in their thirties, were ancient. Later, in the army, I was surprised to discover that some of the officers, many years my senior, were able to stay up with the younger troops during harsh physical training. I realized then that age is really relative: No matter what the chronological age is, a person who has maintained body and mind properly can still remain youthful.

I know many young people who are old before their time and many old people who seem eternally young. Occasionally I take down from my tape library, films of some of the most remarkable old men I have ever seen. Two of the venerable old martial arts masters and Zen practitioners who give me inspiration are Gichin Funakoshi, the father of modern karate, and Morihei Ueshiba, the founder of aikido. Ueshiba was one of the first men to unite spiritual beliefs with technical skill; he realized that the truly critical struggle in man was not physical combat, but rather the internal confrontation with the forces that lead him out of harmony with the spirit of the universe.

Both men were in their late seventies when the demonstration tapes I have were filmed, and I still get goose bumps when

I see these old gentlemen confront several young, strong assailants and dispose of them with unbelievable ease. I admire their technical skills, but more than that, I admire their spirit — they refused to let the infirmities of age affect their body or mind.

Many of the Zen masters I have met or read about were well up in their years, and they all seem to have had some things in common beside their incredible abilities. These venerables prove that an ancient philosophy is still practical for anyone regardless of age: It is knowledge that I wish I had had when I was growing up. Over the years I have attempted to synthesize what I have learned from my reading and from the Zen masters I have met, practices I try to follow myself and that I suggest to my own sons as well as to the youngsters I meet. These are some of these precepts:

• A daily regimen of exercise to keep the body supple, limber, and in good tone. For children I recommend some regular sports activity. Young adults who were active during their childhood should continue with light regular exercise, such as bicycling, swimming, tennis, or golf, with occasional workouts in the gym if feasible. Even when he was nearing ninety years of age, Funakoshi still exercised daily.

• Everything in moderation. As one grows older, it is important to accept the fact that your body and metabolism change. As a young man I indulged in fast foods, snacks, and occasional malts, but I soon realized that I was beginning to slow down a bit during my daily workouts and losing my muscle tone. I knew that I had to be more aware of what I put into my body, and that awareness made a major difference, physically as well as mentally. It's a fact that if most young folk continue their old dietary habits, they will probably gain weight as they age.

• Eat simple but nourishing food at each meal, and never eat until sated. In my view, moderation is the key to a better and longer life. Try to leave the table still feeling a bit hungry. Remember, it takes twenty minutes for your brain to realize you are full, so eat slowly. Another trick to maintaining weight is to eat properly and drink plenty of water.

• Allow for quiet time at some point during the day, a period for introspection and calm or meditation, or perhaps even a short nap to recharge the batteries. I think that even very young people will find a brief nap in the afternoon beneficial.

• Regardless of your age, cherish the company of good friends, because you can be relaxed with them. At the same time, seek out the company of positive-thinking people, because you can learn new ideas from them that will broaden your own horizons. Try to avoid negative thinkers and thoughts.

• Be open to learning new concepts and ideas, regardless of your age. One of my favorite stories is about the scholar who went to visit a famous Zen master to ask how he could achieve enlightenment. As the master poured tea, the scholar, trying to impress the master, talked only about his ideas. The master continued to pour tea into the cup until it overflowed. Noticing this, the scholar said, "Master, the cup is full."

"You are just like this cup," the master said, "You are full of concepts, ideas, and yourself. If you don't empty the cup that is in your mind first, then how can I begin to explain Zen to you?"

• Don't be judgmental. That's easier said than done, especially if you feel you have the advantage of wisdom because you are older than the people you interact with. The Zen masters were far ahead of modern psychiatrists in advancing the notion that one must learn to listen with the third ear in order to hear both what is being said and what you believe the other person is really saying.

• Listen to your heart. The Zen masters believe that intuition, as opposed to intellection and rationalization, is the most direct way of reaching the truth. Thanks to Zen, I have learned to listen with an open mind without interrupting or having a prepared response. I hear the words in my heart and my gut as well as in my head.

• Attitude is everything. I have already discussed how youngsters with problems were able to take charge of their lives by having the proper attitude. Older people need to be just as aware. But there are exceptions. I have an octogenarian friend who has walked five miles a day, rain or shine, since he was a teenager. When he retired some years ago, his family tried to convince him to give up his pedestrian habits, saying he would be better off riding from hole to hole in a golf cart. My friend refused their advice. "Sure I have aches and pains from time to time," he told me. "But if I give up walking for even one day a week, my mind will think I am old. You are what you think you are."

Another longtime friend of mine recently retired when he reached sixty-five. He gave up his customary routines — tennis, swimming, staying in touch with old companions, because he thought they no longer had anything in common — in favor of behaving as he thought he should as a retiree. Now three years into his retirement, he is becoming an old man, his only excitement waiting at the bookstore for the newest bestseller.

• Accept things as they really are and adapt to them. *The Book of Changes (I Ching)* is often considered the perfect example of adaptation. In this book, the recurring theme is one of observing life and going with its flow in order to survive and develop. The basic concept is that anything can be a source of conflict or danger, and, ultimately, violence if it is confronted from the wrong angle or in the wrong manner at the point of its maximum strength. Any and every occurrence can be dealt with by approaching it from the right angle and in the proper manner — that is, at its source, before it can develop full power, or from the sides. When one is confronted with direct force, the *I Ching* advises keeping slightly ahead of or on top of the force, which, like any other concentrated force in creation, will inevitably dissipate.

When I read the above sometime ago, I was learning to surf, and I realized that one of the first things I had to learn in order to ride a wave was to stay just slightly ahead of it. If I moved out too far, I would not be "with it," and I would lose contact with the surging power that had been propelling me along and would probably crush me below the surface. On the other hand, if I allowed the wave to overtake me, I would be "wiped out" by the wave's power, since I would not be "going with the flow."

As I have matured, I realize more and more the wisdom

of some of the Alcoholics Anonymous ideology, of accepting what cannot be changed and knowing the difference. As a result, I function better in my daily life: My thoughts are clearer, my nerves are free from strain, I sleep better at night, and my relationships are more fulfilling.

• Admit your errors. Most of us, regardless of age, find it difficult to admit it when our opinions or judgments are wrong. This is especially true as we get older, due to the widely accepted notion that maturity begets wisdom. It's certainly true that most parents have more life experience than, say, their children or others junior to them. But occasionally they make wrong judgments about people or situations, and it is difficult for them to accept their fallibility. I have learned it is wiser to acknowledge an error at once than to try to defend it. The key is to put your error behind you, and, if your position has created a problem, to take responsibility and help fix the problem.

• There are no excuses for failure. Zen masters believe that peace of mind comes from having done the best you could with your life and not worrying about what you didn't do or don't have. To me, the saddest words I hear are apologies for failure, such as "couldabeen," "shouldabeen," or "mightabeen." Too many youngsters who fail in school or in other endeavors fall back on such apologies, when the truth is, they didn't try hard enough.

• Don't let material things possess you. Difficult as it may seem to accept for young adults who grow up in a materialistic society and want everything at once, the truth is that the things that are most important to a rich life are intangible — health and the love of family and friends. Many people, as they get older, also consider possessions to be more important to their sense of self-worth than the intangible things that really make for a happy and fulfilling life.

• Retain an open mind. Even if you think the experience of your years, regardless of their number, makes you wise, do what has to be done with a disposition open to change or chance. Sometimes what seems to be a detour will turn out to be the fastest way to your goal.

• Continue to make new friends. Always be alert to the possibilities there are in any meeting with a stranger. It can change your life and help you learn. Young people frequently shut themselves off from making new friends because of their own insecurity and the fear that they may not be liked for some reason. At the same time, many older people become curmudgeons, and seal themselves off from strangers, often alienating folk who might enliven their lives. Always remember it's just as easy to make a friend as an enemy.

We have all seen war movies about the famed kamikaze pilots of World War II — Japanese soldiers strapped into what was actually a flying bomb — who flew their small planes into our warships with the certain knowledge that they personally would be annihilated too. Most people think, as I once did, that they were extraordinarily brave, stupid, or drugged before setting off on their missions. After studying Zen, I realize that the Zen concept of dying without regrets means dying with a clear conscience, bravely, with no reluctance, and with complete honor. It's not the quantity of life that's important, it's the quality!

⌣.

I have always been compulsive about being on time for appointments — I don't like making someone wait for me, and I dislike having to wait. Time has always been a precious commodity to me; there never seems to be time enough in a day to accomplish what I consider necessary. I am ever mindful of the Zen adage "Life unfolds on a great sheet called Time, and once finished, it is gone forever."

THE MONK AND
SHANE

Like many Americans, I came to Zen through the martial arts. Actually, the Oriental martial arts began to make their way into the American reality only during World War II. Our soldiers in the Pacific theater encountered these fighting styles, most of them previously unknown to Americans, in combat, and Americans at home learned about them in movie theaters. In a host of American-made films about the Pacific war made during the conflict or in the early 1950s, a moment comes, either in training camp or aboard a transport ship off the coast of an enemy-held island, when the Marines or GIs are briefed about Japanese-style warfare. The Japanese, they are told, don't fight like Americans — or like honorable soldiers in general — but, instead, make use of treacherous, unconventional methods. They hide among the fronds atop palm trees, bury themselves and then leap out of hiding to shoot the unwary in the back, and don't fight fair hand-to-hand: Rather than throwing straight punches, they spin, make unpredictable moves, and use "judo." The martial arts were just one more evil aspect of the wily Japanese enemy. Even unarmed, a Japanese soldier was not to be trusted.

Many American soldiers studied martial arts while in the Pacific and brought their expertise home with them. At the same time, the martial arts were slowly making their way into American films, a reflection of the growing interest in the martial arts in this country. Up until then, the traditional American hero in films, like John Wayne in a John Ford Western, usually stood stock-still with his feet firmly planted on the ground and his fists held honorably in clear view right in front of his square jaw, as he waited for the other guy to throw the first punch.

That heroic stance no longer intimidated or even impressed anyone, but, instead, seemed about as dated as one of those grainy, old Mathew Brady photographs of Civil War soldiers shouldering clumsy muskets. War had changed — violence in all its forms, both international and interpersonal, had changed — and with it, our heroes changed. Today a hero never stands still for long, and when he fights, his hands — and probably also his feet — fly.

It seems like a big change, at least when looked at from the special point of view of the choreography of fight scenes in movies. In a period of just over two decades, the martial arts of the Orient have become solidly embedded in the culture of the United States, or at least in two of the most important expressions of that culture: movies and television.

The film usually cited as the first Hollywood production in which an American star used Oriental fighting techniques is *Blood on the Sun,* from 1945, in which James Cagney uses judo, an art he had actually studied. Martial arts appeared in several other postwar films, usually as a kind of dark secret or arcane skill learned during the war. *Bad Day at Black Rock* from 1955 immediately comes to mind: The one-armed war veteran Spencer Tracy doesn't look like he should be able to take on an entire town, but he is able to do so because of his knowledge of martial arts, presumably learned while he was in the armed forces.

Actually, another film of the mid-fifties seems more important to me: Akira Kurosawa's *The Seven Samurai,* which tells the story of a poor village in Japan that hires seven professional warriors to fight off a gang of bandits. That film's enormous popularity with American audiences has been seen as an early indication of the coming popularity of the martial arts. I think it's important for another reason, too, for it indicated that the gap between the two cultures was merely one of style — the film was called an "Eastern Western," meaning a Japanese version of an American Western. Just four years later, in 1960, it was remade as a "pure" American western: *The Magnificent Seven.*

That film appeared in theaters when I was in Korea and working to earn my black belt. Before arriving at the Osan Air Base, I knew next to nothing about the martial arts; I'd seen some jujitsu in the Peter Lorre *Mr. Moto* films, but that's about all. When I wrote home and told my wife that I was taking karate lessons, she wrote back to me saying that she'd mentioned the lessons to a local police officer, and he'd gotten upset and told her, "My God, have him stop. He'll come home a killer!" That was probably a pretty accurate reflection of American popular opinion of the martial arts at the time: something dangerous, still connected to all those wartime films about the Japanese.

When I came home from Korea, I brought my black belt and also my gi, which was a good thing, since a gi was impossible to buy anywhere in the United States back then.

But things were changing. Mainstream motion pictures

were beginning to feature heroes using martial arts to beef up the action footage. And then, in 1966, a genuine martial artist entered television in the person of Bruce Lee, playing Kato and displaying his flamboyant prowess in *The Green Hornet*. Bruce embellished his style with visually stunning moves, many of them so fast that retakes were necessary.

And then, in the early 1970s, along came the television series *Kung Fu,* starring David Carradine as a Shao-lin monk wandering across the Old West, who defeated all comers with his kung fu and intrigued viewers with his philosophy of nonviolence unless absolutely necessary. Fans of the show didn't learn a lot about the realities of kung fu, but that's hardly surprising, since the term refers to no specific style of martial art and, like so many concepts embedded in ancient Chinese culture, encompasses hundreds of geographical variations and different styles vaguely based on similar ideas. Viewers did, however, have the novel experience of seeing a polite, unassuming monk placed in the kind of dire situations that were once occupied only by the likes of John Wayne. In that sense, the appearance in the Old West of a kung fu monk with his strange garb and unorthodox ways of handling violence was symbolic of something larger: the overall impact on America of the Oriental martial arts and the Zen philosophy behind them.

The martial arts have a special appeal to many people, particularly kids, with all those exciting kicks and punches, the spinning around and leaping. It reminds me of when I was a kid and, since I had no other toys, I used clothespins for my soldiers and cowboys. I had two kinds of clothespins, big and small, and when I set up my battles, my frontier forts and ambushes, I made the big pins the bad guys, the little ones the good guys. That's the way a kid sees the world, and it is consistent with a certain morality: The bad guys are pumped-up bullies eager to do harm; the good guys are smaller and may even appear weaker, but when forced to fight, they do so with courage and overwhelming skill.

The appeal of the martial arts is undeniable, but there's more to them than enthralling spectacle. Exact statements about the philosophies behind the various arts are rare, in large part because Zen itself denies, even defies, any direct definition. But sometimes you can find meaningful words. Judo is a good example. Judo is more sport than martial art, but it's based almost entirely on the martial art of jujitsu, with most of the more "martial" aspects trimmed off, so judo reflects the thinking behind the martial arts. As Jigoro Kano, the founder of judo, claimed, the purpose of judo is not to win contests but to perfect one's mind and body "for the mutual benefit and welfare of all mankind."

That may seem high-sounding, but it's true. It's something all serious martial artists believe in, and it throws light on why the Oriental martial arts were eventually embraced by Americans: The meaning behind the arts slid easily into an important groove in American thinking. The Shao-lin monk of *Kung Fu* is not really so different from the many characters played so adeptly by John Wayne or Alan Ladd as Shane or any of the heroes played by Gary Cooper. What makes an American hero is not how he fights, but what he fights for. That's why it was so easy for the seven samurai of Kurosawa's film to become the seven hard-luck gunslingers in *The Magnificent Seven*.

Martial arts changed the fight choreography but not the plots of American movies. The size of heroes changed, since a martial artist need not be big, and that reality opened the way for female protagonists. In other ways, the martial arts haven't so much changed American films as reflected changes that were already taking place in American attitudes.

In a sense, martial arts suit the themes of contemporary films, which in turn reflect a certain view of modern society. Violence was an aberration for the heroes of old-time Westerns; when the fighting was done, the Colt was put back in the drawer, the Winchester was hung up over the mantel. Martial arts are not that kind of weapon: They dwell forever within the practitioner, making him ever ready and thus well-suited to our sense of a world of constant threats. The martial arts are also personal — each fighter stands alone — reflecting, I suppose, our diminished faith in institutions. They also provide a special kind of individuality to lead actors, in which a style of fighting becomes an expression of personal character.

There is in addition a more subtle aspect to the introduction of martial arts to American films, one that is often overlooked. Learning a martial art is not like learning to play baseball or to shoot a gun — it's not a skill picked up and practiced at odd times. A martial art can't be truly learned without having a profound effect on the student. To learn a martial art requires as much use of the brain as the muscles. Behind each art is a philosophy that is necessarily applied not just to the performance of the martial art but to the performance of life. "For the mutual benefit and welfare of all mankind" — the phrase is important. True martial artists, when teaching or training, realize that every move they make is a philosophy not of violence, but of life.

Many of today's popular actors are real martial artists, which means that behind each one is a story of learning and adapting, a personal story about important choices. I like to think that the martial arts have given us a generation of actors who reflect on what they're doing, on the messages they're sending young people. I know I think long and hard about it. I want to live up to the heroes of my youth, to their ideals. Those ideals are meant to be applied both in films and in real life, and I want to update those ideals for today's kids. If anyone chooses to imitate me, I want it to be for his or her benefit, as well as for that of the rest of our nation.

THE WAY OF
THE WARRIOR

According to the Dalai Lama, all the teachings of Buddhism
can be distilled into two sentences: "If you can,
help others; if you cannot do that, at least do
not harm them."

In the past as today, Zen monasteries are usually located in
the countryside, up in the mountains and far from densely
populated areas. There were two good reasons for that: First,
locating the monastery in the mountains put the monks in
close contact with nature, with the realities of life unfettered
by the rules and customs, by the many forms of control, that
invariably accompany big populations of people. There's a lot
of artificiality involved in living in urban centers, and Zen is
about avoiding the artificial. The second reason is tied to the
realities of history: Being in the mountains and away from
cities helped the monks avoid problems with centers of power,
with political authorities of all kinds. The philosophy of Zen,

which tended to apply a highly critical eye to the manipulations of worldly power, didn't always sit well with the men in charge of running countries, and it was a good idea to stay clear of them. It's also true that Buddhism, of which Zen is a sect, began in India and was therefore a new and "foreign" religion in such places as China and Japan. Simply by existing among the people and offering an alternative view of life, Zen called into question the veneration of emperors and lesser lights. Zen monks were valued for their learning, becoming active in literary and artistic circles and even occupying positions of political influence. And in countries habitually torn by internal strife and power struggles, involvement in politics at any level and on any side could and did lead to conflict. For these reasons, the emperors of both China and Japan made repeated attempts to eliminate the Zen Buddhist influence. The most famous such attempt took place in 845, when the Chinese emperor Wu-tsung carried out a great persecution of all Buddhists and Zen practitioners. That effort, like all those before and after, ultimately failed in its goal. In both countries Zen eventually emerged as an important sect, partly because of its innate vitality and partly because it stayed isolated in the mountains.

Zen practitioners have always been in intimate touch with the natural world, and this close contact with nature shows up in much of the thinking behind Zen: close observation of nature, of plants and animals, rocks and rivers, can lead to important insights about life and also helps in meditation. Many Zen sayings are based on the observation of nature. One of Bruce Lee's favorites was "In the landscape of spring there is neither better nor worse. The flowering branches grow, some short, some long." Bruce applied that saying to his philosophy of the martial arts: According to him, there was no one superior style of martial arts; all of them had something of value to offer.

Where there are mountains, there are mountain streams, and many Zen sayings refer to the fluid movement of water. In fact, that movement — or the movement of something floating along on moving water — illustrates a basic concept of Zen. Water flows freely; a ball tossed into a mountain stream floats along, bobbing and moving from side to side, without hesitation, without interruption. It's obvious that the ball isn't thinking about where it's going, and it's equally obvious that the ball is making good progress along the stream. It's as though the ball had its eyes closed and moved without reflection along the current of the stream, finding the right way naturally. And from there it's a simple step to seeing the flowing current as the stream or road of life, and the ball then becomes you or me, making our way through life.

Zen was the foundation of the martial arts in feudal Asia — Japan, Okinawa, and China. When some of those countries decreed that only royalty and warriors could carry weapons, many of the Zen sects retreated to secluded places and began to develop ways the unarmed man could successfully defend himself against an armed opponent using any weapon of opportunity. The nunchakus, for example, were developed from flails used to grind wheat. The jumping kicks, which are a feature of many martial arts systems today, were used to enable a man on the ground to jump high enough and with sufficient power to propel a mounted warrior off his horse.

In time, Zen, which had its origins in Chinese Buddhism, was embraced in Japan and became the philosophy behind bujutsu, the military arts of the samurai, the way of the warrior. Many of the attributes of a samurai warrior — the enormous self-discipline, the austerity, the indifference to physical discomfort, pain, even death — are taken directly from the study of Zen. The samurai were professional warriors, men trained to fight and die, so it was only natural that they were drawn to a philosophy that offered detachment from the physical world, a way of conquering the self so thoroughly and absolutely that death could be faced without fear. But, of course, even the samurai preferred life, and when they sought out Zen masters — when they rode up into the mountains to a monastery to learn Zen — they were hoping to acquire techniques that would help them stay alive in the swirl and confusion of battle. They were hoping to learn to move like that ball in the stream — without reflective thought and by intuition alone.

The most important contribution made by Japanese Zen to the warriors of the time was the development of intuitive powers, for the Zen masters believed that intuition was a more direct way of reaching the truth than reflection. In fact, although Zen is rightly associated with meditation, it often seems to take the side of action rather than reflection. This is expressed in the Zen maxim of "going straight ahead without stopping, without looking back." And that means responding instantaneously, through intuition. By developing intuition, the samurai could respond immediately to danger without hesitation, without pausing to reflect, much less have any doubts about the outcome of battle.

Then, as now, what the Zen masters said was that intuitive understanding cannot be taught but is, instead, awakened in the mind after many years of dedicated training, discipline, and meditation. Certainly the most impressive example of this is the Zen archer who hits his mark with his eyes closed. Magic or trickery has nothing to do with it: He releases his arrow with intuition, and behind that intuition are years of training and meditation, an enormous inner discipline.

The way of the warrior is therefore based on intuition, his mind responding like the ball in the mountain stream, his movements fluid and unhesitating.

The samurai warriors, of course, applied this concept to a life that was in many ways alien to Zen. The life of a samurai was ruled by a code of loyalty and obedience to a feudal lord and was imbued with violence, thus clearly at odds with the basic tenets or precepts of Zen Buddhism, the first of which was originally "no taking of life." In a similar way, applying intuitive thinking to our modern lives can seem awkward, even immoral. It seems that we have to ponder every move we make, constantly assessing our motives, questioning ourselves, and always looking back, sometimes with regret, while at the same time looking forward, very often with anxiety.

But as the Zen masters taught, intuition is not learned but, instead, awakens within us, and it comes not from the tap of some magic wand but as the result of discipline. As a martial artist I know that many of my most impressive feats — times when I've impressed myself as much as the spectators — happened when I responded effortlessly, when my body had moved long before my mind had caught up with the situation I was facing. In such cases, the power of my training and my discipline — all those long hours spent repeating the same movements over and over — came to the fore with a speed far beyond any thoughts from my brain. And as a husband and father, friend, brother, and son — as a human being living among others — I know that many of the most important moments in my personal life were when I responded not in accordance with what I had reasoned to be the best course of action but when I acted in accordance with the urging of my gut or heart. My mother used to tell me and my brothers, "Listen to your heart. It has much wisdom to share." In such cases, what comes to the fore is something stronger than intellectual reflection, and something far more valuable and potent.

That kind of intuition, those movements of inner success, come from self-confidence. If you want to move successfully along the current of life, you must trust yourself and help yourself, which means giving yourself positive reinforcement. Never allow yourself to nurture negative thoughts. Think positively, plan, and do what has to be done. If you plant the right seed, it will grow into your destiny if you feed it and nurture it. The fruit will ripen in season. But waiting and hoping are not enough: Good outcomes require good actions.

The self-confidence to do these things comes from discipline and learning. As you apply these to difficult challenges, you will acquire the personal strength to go on to other successes. There will be times when you don't know what to do, when your head dictates one course of action, your gut another. Which to follow? Always go with your gut. If this results in a setback, so what? You can be thwarted, but not defeated. You can be delayed, but not devastated.

Whatever you've accomplished — and the more difficult it was, the better — becomes part of your life. Your accomplishments help make the concept of success part of the fabric of your being. They reduce the concept of failure to a harmless abstraction. Eventually, your intuition — the decisions to which your mind, heart, or your gut leaps — will spring forward from a platform of success. You will have disciplined your mind — and your heart — to intuit the right way. And as you go forward from success to success, you'll realize that you are no longer thinking of finish lines, but of new goals, new challenges, and new horizons. The stream just flows on and on.

You have to handle each day's necessary assignments, but you can do so with a disposition open to chance or change. Sometimes what seems like an awkward detour can turn out to be the fastest way to your goal. Don't hesitate: Like any meeting with a stranger, something new may well indicate the next stage in your development, the next part of the road to travel.

But don't expect instant success, don't give in to the weakness of pride, which almost always leads to carelessness. And never give up too soon. No matter what other people tell you, you can always push yourself a little farther, and that short distance may prove to be more than enough.

And don't give in to worry. Worrying and fretting are wrong: They waste energy and clog your creativity, making it impossible for you to see your problems clearly. The truth is that even with a clear blueprint for the future in your mind — and with success in your subconscious — you may experience times when you're too busy to see ahead clearly, when day-to-day responsibilities become so overwhelming that you feel you're losing track of your goals. Don't worry even then, for something will happen to remind you.

Sometimes (I know this has happened to me, so I imagine it happens to all of us at some time or other) you find yourself off alone somewhere — maybe up in the mountains, maybe even by a running stream, maybe standing on a stretch of dry desert sand — and looking at the world, at that piece of natural world in front of you. Suddenly all the artificiality drops away, and everything suddenly seems so easy, the things to be done all kind of fall into place and make sense in a new way, the road ahead through your life then seems open and clear, with nothing standing in the way. But then you turn around, get back in your car, and soon enough find yourself back in town, with all the other voices and all the other pressures, and you lose sight of that open road. But it's always there inside you, and if you remain true to yourself, to your chosen discipline, and to those you love, you'll discover that you are moving steadily right along that road all the time, finding your way effortlessly, just as if you were in the current, just as if you already knew the way.

RECOGNIZING
YOURSELF

Some people, mostly close friends and family, call me Carlos, and it doesn't bother me in the least. The simple truth is that throughout all of my childhood, all the way up to when I got married, my name was Carlos. That's what everyone called me, from my mother to the teachers at school to all my friends. My birth certificate reads "Carlos Ray Norris." The Carlos comes from the Reverend Carlos Berry, my family's local minister back in Ryan, Oklahoma; Ray was my father's name. I came by the name Chuck while I was in the air force. One of the guys in my barracks in boot camp asked me what Carlos meant in English. I told him it was the same as Charles, and he immediately took to calling me Chuck. The nickname somehow stuck. I don't remember ever giving much thought to that slight change in my name. It didn't seem all that important, and when I came back from my tour of duty in Korea I brought home the new name in addition to my gi, my black belt, and my new sense of myself, which came with having achieved the black belt.

So I suppose you could say that that first black belt drew a kind of dividing line across the early period of my life. On one side of the line was Carlos, on the other was Chuck; on one side was a young man whose future was still primarily in other people's hands — parents and teachers, employers and high-ranking officers, all kinds of people telling him what to do — and on the other side was a young man who'd finally learned to take hold of his future. Or maybe that's an exaggeration: I'd say only that by the time I came back from Korea, I'd seen that it was possible to take hold of my life. I'd taken one step and was eager for more.

It didn't take long. Within a few years I had my own school, with a sign outside reading "Chuck Norris Karate." Then, in 1964, I began competing in karate tournaments. My goal was simple: to win tournaments and get public exposure in order to attract more students. I was twenty-four years old when I started and was thus older than most of the other competitors, and, of course, I was unknown. I'd drive to the site of the tournament, usually piled into a car together with a group of my students, get on line with the others, sign my name and register, and then pay my fee to enter the competition. By the time my name was called, I'd be concentrating, visualizing my next fight, so I never really heard whatever response those early crowds gave my name. Some people in the stands always applaud every name, just to be polite, and sometimes my students or other friends or family would call out encouragement to me, but I don't think I ever heard them or was really aware of the sound — at least not in the beginning, by which I mean the first few years.

But the time did finally come when the response to my name being called was audible, even to me, even through my wall of solid concentration. People knew who I was, strangers I had never even seen let alone met were applauding my name. It's a strange sensation, and since I've always been shy and retiring, it wasn't easy to get accustomed to. And then the moment came when that first unknown someone stepped forward out of the background and asked for my autograph. I can't remember the first time that happened, but it was back when I was known only as a martial artist. Fans would come up before or after a match and ask me to sign the program or my school's patch or any piece of paper they happened to have, and, although I was sometimes embarrassed by the attention, I was always pleased. And I'd sign "Chuck Norris," which was the name of an up-and-coming karate champion, a well-known instructor with his own school and a following of black belts.

I was known for my kicks, particularly my famous spinning back kick. I was also known for my stamina and my stoicism, characteristics that may have attracted special attention because I was often competing against younger men. And I was also known for other traits and attributes. Along with applause, I began getting something else back from the spectators around me: a reflection of my personal self, a new "portrait" of the man known as Chuck Norris, a portrait I didn't always recognize at first glance.

I didn't always recognize it because I hadn't been aware of creating it. I've never been flamboyant or showy. In point of fact, I don't think I've ever done anything on purpose to make myself stand out, but there I was in that certain spotlight. I had wanted that attention, of course — I had set out to get it — and by winning tournaments I was indeed attracting new students, which had been my original goal. But I was also becoming a public figure, at least within the world of the martial arts, and that was something I hadn't planned on or even anticipated. People saw more than my kicks and my stamina when they watched me compete: They saw my movements and "read" them in ways I hadn't anticipated. What was to me only another kick, just part of my arsenal, was to them an expression of my character, a window onto some aspect of the person I am. If I joked with a competitor before a match or said something self-effacing, it would come back to me as part of that new public image: I learned I was considered forthright and easygoing. Some fighters, of course, exploit the situation and put on a show of being bellicose maniacs in order to intimidate their opponents and delight their fans while outraging others. It had never occurred to me to act a part or to change myself to augment my public persona; I was just being me (and trying not to get my nose broken too many times).

That period was an important lesson to me. I've always tried to live by my ideals, to live up to my ideals, to be the best I am capable of being and then to go beyond that. I looked on those ideals as being central to taking control of my life, to taking positive steps to achieve my goals. My ideals were also important to me as a teacher, since I wanted to give my students, especially the young ones, a valid and enduring role model, something they could look up to and believe in. In response to my fans, to the fact that people were watching me, I realized that I was coming to stand for something and that I was in control of what that something would be. In truth, I alone was responsible for what it would be.

There's a Zen saying according to which knowledge is the reward of action. My actions in karate tournaments rewarded me with a kind of self-knowledge, or at least an awareness of what that self had promise of becoming, and by the time I officially retired from tournament karate in 1974, after a decade of active competition, I had crossed what might be considered another line in my life. On one side was a man eager to achieve success; on the other was a man whose idea of success had expanded, a man eager to explore all possibilities.

But there is another truth that must be said. I reached that line in my life also by way of hammer blows, by way of passing through a personal gauntlet of crises and pain. You can read in a book that "the way to true understanding must lead through personal experience and suffering," and you nod your head in silent agreement; but when you're in the middle of that very real suffering, you may decide that you'd just as soon do without any "understanding" that might be coming your way on the other side. My brother Wieland's death in Vietnam affected my sense of self far more than any applause or glowing write-ups. My affable character and lightning-quick back kicks had been unable to do anything to protect him when he most needed it. I hadn't been there, and for a long time after his death, I didn't want to be anywhere at all.

There were also personal problems, both with my business and my family. I reached a time when I wasn't sure I wanted to be a husband anymore — after all, I'd gotten married when I was just a kid and had never known any other life. I was weary of the constant struggle of running a business. For a short while I lost sense of who I was and what I really wanted to do. When I wasn't actively fighting off negative thoughts, I was bored and restless.

Then Steve McQueen asked me why I hadn't tried acting, and the result was a new career.

It certainly wasn't easy, and certainly didn't happen overnight. Becoming Chuck Norris the actor seemed to mean leaving behind the karate expert and the teacher. My famous stoicism was itself a drawback. I had taught myself to quietly endure pain and tension, anger or elation, without giving away even the faintest expression of those emotions. Success on the mat often depends on hiding all such emotions from your opponent; success in acting usually calls for just the opposite, the visible and believable expression of one's emotions. When I started my career as an actor, I suddenly had to learn how to bring all those feelings to the surface and then manipulate them. It was hard and more than a little disconcerting.

Eventually, however, I found a way to use my skills as a karate expert in the creation of movies, and I did so by realizing that conflict is usually the basic essence of a dramatic scene, and conflict was something with which I was abundantly familiar. I also learned to apply my visualizing techniques to acting; just as I had once visualized a match, I learned to visualize each scene of a film.

In the end, I also didn't have to leave behind my experience as a teacher. Actually, you could say that I just expanded my classroom, since my goal as an actor has come to be much the same as my goal as a karate instructor: to give young people in particular a positive image they can believe in and follow. And, of course, I was the same person as an actor as I was in real life. Unlike many people going into show business I never considered changing my name. It wasn't just because I didn't want to lose any fans; I knew that as an actor I would always be Chuck Norris.

I based my version of a true American role model, a hero, on the movies I'd watched as a kid, in particular the Westerns starring John Wayne. In the 1970s, when I started my career in films, there weren't many heroes of that type on the screen; it was instead a troubled period of grim skepticism, a time without heroes, precisely because no one seemed to believe in anything anymore.

Except for me. I believed in what my life had taught me, in

the knowledge I had been awarded through action and in the understanding I had come by through experiencing and overcoming pain and loss. Nothing has ever happened to me that could make me ever doubt the validity of what I was taught as a child, regarding both the larger ideals of this country and the smaller ones — the opportunities available to anyone who honestly strives to achieve his goals. Then, as now, I believe in those ideals, and I used them to break the long silence of the 1970s.

My first films were not well received by critics, and even now I wince when I see myself in some of those early pictures. Some people dismissed them as "chop-socky" flicks, which they really weren't, although it took time to make that clear to everyone.

While the critics may not have enjoyed my first films, the American public certainly did. The films made money, and I knew from the response of my fans that I was getting my message across.

I had always wanted to do something in honor of Wieland. I had always wanted to in some way make a valid response to his death. The time finally came in 1983. Even then, a full decade after the end of our involvement in Vietnam, few American film makers dared touch the subject of the Vietnam War. They were still divided or fearful of treading on divisions still existing among Americans. I believed otherwise, and I had something I wanted to say.

The resulting film, *Missing in Action,* was an enormous success. I'll never forget going to an opening in a theater in Westwood, California. At the climax of the film, the entire audience came to its feet, applauding and cheering. That film's sequel was not long in coming, and it, too, was enormously popular. I knew people were listening to what I was saying.

After *Missing in Action 2*, I made *Code of Silence,* and with that film I finally won applause even from the major critics (and the reminder from Burt Reynolds that "you're only as good as your last film").

Just as I never thought of altering myself to match my public persona when I was a karate competitor, I've never considered doing anything to change my image on screen. I perform only parts that fit what I believe in. Aside from my personal ideals and taste, I do this because I know that kids make up a large percentage of my fans, and they pay little attention to the name of the character I'm supposed to be playing and see me only as Chuck Norris. They recognize my face and expect me to act in a certain way. I have no intention of disappointing them.

Kids are by no means my only fans, of course, and I also try to provide meaningful entertainment for adult audiences. Many adults in America need someone with whom they can identify, someone self-reliant and unafraid, someone who is symbolic of what we all know to be right. At least for a period of the film, they can revel in the character's efforts to combat wrong; and his eventual success, his victory over evil, may well serve to give people a needed boost and perhaps also a gentle reminder of our shared ideals.

Many of the young people who watch my films today have no idea that I was once a karate teacher and champion. They think I'm just an actor who's good at martial arts. And these days, of course, I'm probably best known for my television series, *Walker, Texas Ranger,* and I know that some of its fans don't associate me with the martial arts at all; they see different aspects of my character. There are some differences in the character I play on television: in a sense, Walker can be seen as a further refinement of the character I've been playing over all these years, reflecting changes in myself as an actor and a person. But that character is still me, and if audiences see his movements, his gestures, as expressions of a point of view, of a moral stance, they're absolutely right.

For that is only a reflection of Zen, of the central meaning of action, of what we actually do with our lives and how we deal with the people around us. I've had the pleasure of hearing myself applauded, first as a karate competitor and then as a symbol. Such applause is available to all of us, for all of us can control the image we project to others, whether on a movie screen or across a room. By treating other people with respect, by controlling our actions and words, we convey an outward image of our inner selves. If we are honest, that image will be true. You should recognize yourself in the image others have of you; it should be an image you yourself would respect.

As I say, some of my old friends and family still call me Carlos. It's a form of affection, a gentle reminder that they knew me "way back when," back when few people knew who I really was, including even myself.

IN MEMORIAM

My younger brother Wieland died more than twenty-five years ago, in 1970, in the month of June, one month before his twenty-eighth birthday. He died in Vietnam, cut down by the Vietcong while leading his squad through enemy-held territory. At a certain point, he must have suspected something, because he motioned for his men to stay put while he went ahead alone to scout the trail. He spotted an enemy patrol setting up an ambush, yelled back to warn his men, and then the shooting started. That is what happened, as it was related to me later, and I have gone over those moments in my mind endlessly, seeing it like a scene in a movie, the yelling, the gestures, working it over and over to get it straight, to reach some kind of understanding, but also, I know, in the hope that it will somehow reach a different climax. But it always ends the same way, and Wieland, my brother, is always dead.

Fumio Demura, one of the most important men in martial arts in the United States, was holding a tournament at the Japanese Deer Park in California, with lots of exciting bouts with contestants from all over the country. I was acting as referee and was in the middle of judging a match when I heard my name being called over the loudspeaker. The voice said I had an urgent telephone call. And then I was listening to the voice of my mother-in-law, Evelyn, crying so uncontrollably that the only way she could get the words out of her mouth was to blurt them out, hard and fast. That's how I learned that Wieland was dead.

He was born on July 12, 1943, just about the dead center of World War II. In fact, my father was drafted a few months later, and less than a year after that, we got a telegram saying that he was listed as missing in action. Three months went by like that, without hearing anything, but then he came home. He'd been wounded, and he came home from the war with a drinking problem that was eventually to hurt all of us.

Aaron, my youngest brother, was born in November 1951. By then my father was rarely around, and when he was at home, he was almost always drunk. Since we couldn't afford a baby-sitter and my mother had to work, I had to rush home from school every day to look after my two younger brothers. I can remember taking care of both of them, and as I stood there in the Japanese Deer Park with that phone in my hand, I remembered rocking Wieland to sleep in my arms.

I had nothing of greater value than my brother. I would have given anything not to lose him, and there was nothing I could do to get him back. That sunny June day was the saddest day of my life.

Consolation comes in many forms, all of them meaningful and helpful to a degree, and families, even small ones, can generate enormous amounts of powerful support to deal with such a terrible loss. The first piercing grief eventually becomes a kind of ever-present sorrow that doesn't seem to want to go away ever, but then it does; or, rather, it grows into something else, something you know you can live with, although at the same time you know you'll never forget.

Wieland, Aaron, and I took care of each other the way brothers do, in a way that doesn't always make sense to other people but that lays down meanings and understandings that last a lifetime. We grew up without a father, and that made us closer, sensitive to each other's needs, aware of each other in important ways. And I was the eldest. I wouldn't say necessarily that my two brothers followed me, but I always had to go first to show them the way, for that comes naturally. As the biggest and the oldest, I saw them as my responsibility, and also as my best friends, people to look out for and teach. I was proud the day Wieland earned his black belt. He was my brother, and I had taught him what I knew and loved.

They didn't follow my lead as far as the military goes. I'd been in the air force, but they both enlisted in the army, first Aaron and then, a few weeks later, Wieland. They both wound up in the same camp for basic training, and at night they used to sneak out and meet in a corner of the camp behind Aaron's compound. Strictly speaking, that was against the rules, of course, but I know why they did it, and had I been there, I would have joined them. Brothers always have a lot to say to each other. As it happened, Aaron was at a base in Korea when Wieland died. They gave him emergency leave to come home for the funeral.

The funeral itself was a form of consolation. Several years later, when I made *Missing in Action* and *Missing in Action 2*, I had just cause to think about the fact that we were lucky to know where Wieland was buried, unlike the families of the men who were then still unaccounted for.

I've had a lot of time to think about Wieland's death. I know why he was in Vietnam; after all, he and I, along with Aaron, grew up together, learning and discussing the same ideals, which included patriotism and the willingness to give all we had for our country. He died doing the right thing, making the right gesture: going ahead alone to make the way safe for the men who were depending on him.

In that sense, the pain of my loss has always been mixed with an equally heartbreaking sense of pride. In doing what he did, Wieland was doing what I had taught him, not just with words but with actions. Going in first, which comes naturally to an older brother, can become an act of heroism for a soldier. And in an even larger sense — the sense of going to confront possible death — Wieland went ahead of me, just as surely as he went ahead of his men. He went first that day, and now I, who once rocked him, am still here. But when I repeat his gestures of heroism, when I make films or shows about men who sacrifice for the benefit of others, who risk their lives for what they believe in, I am only following the example of my brother. Zen likes circles: Life must go on.

A CHUCK NORRIS PROFILE

1965

Los Angeles All-Star
  Championships
  Grand Champion
California State Championships
  Grand Champion
Winter Nationals (San Jose)
  Grand Champion

1966

International Karate
  Championships (Long
  Beach)
  Middleweight Champion
National Winter Karate
  Championships (San Jose)
  Grand Champion
International Karate Federation
  Championships
  First Place

1967

North America Championships
  (New York)
  Grand Champion
All-American Championships
  (New York)
  Grand Champion
National Tournament of
  Champions (Cleveland)
  Grand Champion
American Tang Soo Do
  Championships (Washington,
  D.C.)
  Grand Champion
Central Valley Championships
  (Stockton, California)
  Grand Champion
International Karate
  Championships (Long
  Beach)
  Middleweight Champion
  Grand Champion

Korean-Style Kata Champion
Tournament of Champions
(New York)
Grand Champion
All-American Open Karate
Championships (New York)
Lightweight Champion
Grand Champion
International Karate
Championships (Long
Beach)
Grand Champion

1968

U.S. Championships (Dallas)
Lightweight Champion
All-American Karate
Championships (New York)
Grand Champion
Long Beach Internationals
Grand Champion
World Professional Karate
Championships (New York)
Middleweight Champion
Second American Tang Soo Do
Invitational (Washington,
D.C.)
Grand Champion

Hawaii–U.S. Mainland
Competition (Honolulu)
member of winning team
East Coast vs. West Coast
Championships (New York)
member of West Coast team

1969

World Professional Karate
Championships (New York)
Middleweight Champion
International Karate
Championships (Long
Beach)
Korean-Style Kata Champion
(Note: From 1967 to 1969,
Chuck Norris's Black Belt
Karate Team went undefeated
in 80 straight matches.)

1970

U.S. Team Championships
(Long Beach)
member of winning team

FILMS

The Wrecking Crew, 1969
Return of the Dragon, 1973
Breaker! Breaker!, 1977
Good Guys Wear Black, 1977
A Force of One, 1979
The Octagon, 1980
An Eye for an Eye, 1981
Silent Rage, 1982

Forced Vengeance, 1982
Lone Wolf McQuade, 1983
Missing in Action, 1984
Missing in Action 2 — The Beginning, 1985
Code of Silence, 1985
Invasion U.S.A., 1985
Delta Force, 1986
Firewalker, 1986
Braddock: Missing in Action III, 1988
Hero and the Terror, 1988
Delta Force 2 — Operation Stranglehold, 1990
The Hitman, 1991
Sidekicks, 1993
Hellbound, 1994
Top Dog, 1995

TELEVISION

Walker: Texas Ranger, 1993–